Indigeneity in the Courtroom

Indigenous Peoples and Politics

FRANKE WILMER, *General Editor*

Inventing Indigenous Knowledge
Archaeology, Rural Development,
and the Raised Field Rehabilitation
Project in Bolivia
Lynn Swartley

**The Globalization of
Contentious Politics**
The Amazonian Indigenous
Rights Movement
Pamela L. Martin

**Cultural Intermarriage in
Southern Appalachia**
Cherokee Elements in Four Selected
Novels by Lee Smith
Kateřina Prajnerovã

**Storied Voices in Native
American Texts**
Harry Robinson, Thomas King, James
Welch, and Leslie Marmon Silko
Blanca Schorcht

**On the Streets and in the
State House**
American Indian and Hispanic Women
and Environmental Policymaking in
New Mexico
Diane-Michele Prindeville

**Chief Joseph, Yellow Wolf, and
the Creation of Nez Perce History
in the Pacific Northwest**
Robert R. McCoy

**National Identity and the Conflict
at Oka**
Native Belonging and Myths of
Postcolonial Nationhood in Canada
Amelia Kalant

**Native American and Chicano/a
Literature of the American Southwest**
Intersections of Indigenous Literature
Christina M. Hebebrand

The Present Politics of the Past
Indigenous Legal Activism and
Resistance to (Neo)Liberal
Governmentality
Seán Patrick Eudaily

The Ecological Native
Indigenous Peoples' Movements and
Eco-Governmentality in Colombia
Astrid Ulloa

Spiraling Webs of Relation
Movements Toward an Indigenist
Criticism
Joanne R. DiNova

Negotiating Claims
The Emergence of Indigenous
Land Claim Negotiation Policies in
Australia, Canada, New Zealand, and
the United States
Christa Scholtz

Collective Rights of Indigenous Peoples
Identity-Based Movement of Plain Indigenous in Taiwan
Jolan Hsieh

The State and Indigenous Movements
Keri E. Iyall Smith

Speaking with Authority
The Emergence of the Vocabulary of First Nations' Self Government
Michael W. Posluns

Media and Ethnic Identity
Hopi Views on Media, Identity, and Communication
Ritva Levo-Henriksson

The State, Removal and Indigenous Peoples in the United States and Mexico, 1620–2000
Claudia B. Haake

Indigeneity in the Courtroom
Law, Culture, and the Production of Difference in North American Courts
Jennifer A. Hamilton

Indigeneity in the Courtroom

Law, Culture, and the Production of Difference in North American Courts

Jennifer A. Hamilton

Routledge
Taylor & Francis Group
New York   London

First published 2009
by Routledge
270 Madison Ave, New York, NY 10016

Simultaneously published in the UK
by Routledge
2 Park Square, Milton Park, Abingdon, Oxon OX14 4RN

Routledge is an imprint of the Taylor & Francis Group, an informa business

© 2009 Taylor & Francis

Typeset in Sabon by IBT Global.

Library of Congress Cataloging in Publication Data
Hamilton, Jennifer Anne, 1971-
Indigeneity in the courtroom : law, culture, and the production of difference in North American courts / By Jennifer A. Hamilton. -- 1st ed.
p. cm. — (Indigenous peoples and politics)
Includes bibliographical references and index.
ISBN 978-0-415-97904-7
1. Indians of North America—Legal status, laws, etc.—North America. 2. Conduct of court proceedings—North America. 3. Justice, Administration of—North America. 4. Indigenous peoples—Ethnic identity. I. Title.

KDZ495.H36 2008
347.7'0504--dc22
2008023485

ISBN10: 0-415-97904-8 (hbk)
ISBN10: 0-203-88683-6 (ebk)

ISBN13: 978-0-415-97904-7 (hbk)
ISBN13: 978-0-203-88683-0 (ebk)

For Jacob

Contents

Acknowledgments   xi

1   Introduction: Tracking Indigeneity in the Courtroom   1

2   Banishment: Indigenous Justice and Indigenous Difference in
    Washington v. Roberts and Guthrie   7

3   Healing the Bishop: Sexual Violence, Consent, and the Legal
    Erasure of Colonial History in *R. v. O'Connor*   24

4   Resettling Musqueam Park: Property, Culture, and Difference
    in *Glass v. Musqueam Indian Band*   45

5   Of Caucasoids and Kin: Kennewick Man, Race, and Genetic
    Indigeneity in *Bonnichsen v. United States*   71

Notes   89
Bibliography   99
Index   127

Acknowledgments

During the past ten years, I have had the pleasure of working with countless colleagues who have served as mentors, interlocutors, and supporters. Chief among them are the members of my dissertation committee at Rice University: Jim Faubion, Lynne Huffer, Hannah Landecker, and George Marcus. Each brought a unique perspective to this work, and I deeply appreciate their commitment to, and continued enthusiasm about, this project.

I would like to recognize the many people who were willing to share their personal stories with me while I conducted fieldwork in Vancouver and Seattle. This project would never have been possible without you and the numerous lawyers, judges, activists, and volunteers who gave of their time. I would especially like to thank Fay Blaney and Audrey Huntley of the Aboriginal Women's Action Network (AWAN).

I am indebted to Bruce Miller, who so generously shared his time and ideas throughout the course of this project. By opening doors for me both inside and outside the academic community, he expanded my intellectual horizons and helped this book evolve into its current form.

My appreciation goes to my wonderful students at Rice University, the University of Houston-Clear Lake, and Hampshire College. They have helped me see things from fresh perspectives, and their enthusiasm always reinvigorates me. Our classroom discussions have contributed in a fundamental way to the shaping of this project.

The following people have offered me assistance, advice, and inspiration throughout this process, and I am deeply in their debt: Carolyn Babula, Joy Bryant, Caroline Butler, Angela Cameron, Jessica Cattelino, Anne Cohn, Dara Culhane, Eve Darian-Smith, Hülya Demirdirek, J. Kent Fitzpatrick, Andrea Frolic, Nia Georges, Patty Ginn, Maya Grosul, Alison Hamilton, Marlee Hamilton, Neil Hamilton, Hank Hancock, Randy Hanson, Laura Helper-Ferris, Mette Hjort, Chuck Jackson, Berkeley Kaite, Lamia Karim, Chris Kelty, Jennifer Kramer, Shannon Leonard, Amy McGuire, Jane McMillan, Kathryn Milun, Nahal Naficy, Kristin Norget, Valerie Olson, Participants in the 5th Annual Law & Humanities Junior Scholars Workshop (especially commentators Beth Povinelli and Sarah Harding), Kris Peterson, Aimee Placas, Deepa Reddy, Brian Riedel,

Pat Seed, Rich Sharp, Jacob Speaks, Carole Speranza, Kayte Young, and Nancy Zasada.

The following institutions generously provided funding at various stages of this project: Social Sciences and Humanities Research Council of Canada (SSHRC), the SSHRC Federalism and Federations Program, the Wenner-Gren Foundation for Anthropological Research, and the Department of Anthropology and the Office of Research and Graduate Studies at Rice University. Research support for Chapter 5 was in part provided by the National Human Genome Research Institute (NHGRI) Grant 5 P41 HG03083-O1A1 through the Center for Medical Ethics and Health Policy at Baylor College of Medicine.

Special thanks go to my editor at Routledge, Ben Holtzman, and to series editor Franke Wilmer, for their support.

This book is dedicated to Jacob Speaks who deserves all the love and accolades the world has to offer.

1 Introduction
Tracking Indigeneity in the Courtroom

This introduction briefly outlines the terrain of "indigeneity in the courtroom" and locates how indigenous difference is produced in North American courts.[1] The central question of this book is when and how does indigeneity in its various iterations—cultural, social, political, economic, even genetic—matter in a legal sense? When does it not? Indigeneity here references not the specific ontologies and epistemologies of peoples living throughout Native North America, but rather the political, economic and legal articulations of indigenous difference (and the discursive and material effects of these articulations) in postcolonial settler nations.[2]

Indigeneity in the Courtroom is not a comprehensive comparative work that considers the similarities and differences among entire bodies of law. Rather, it focuses on the legal deployment of indigenous difference within a particular spatial and temporal scope—the Native Northwest Coast in the late twentieth and early twenty-first centuries. Relying on ethnographic methods and modes of analysis, I trace the dimensions of indigeneity through close readings of four legal cases, each of which raises a different set of questions about law, culture, and the production of difference. I look at the realm of law, seeking to understand how indigeneity is legally produced and to apprehend its broader political and economic implications.

In each of the four cases, legal actors deploy the idiom of indigeneity in order to make claims to rights, to property, and to political standing. Not only are assertions of indigeneity in these legal cases extremely varied (this book examines cases involving violent and sexual crimes, land disputes, and the disposition of human remains), but the actors making these assertions are also not always indigenous subjects. I argue that despite the purportedly novel nature of these cases, indigeneity in the courtroom is the most recent expression of a powerful colonialist legal tradition whose legacy continues to shape contemporary claims. Through a critical examination of these cases, I seek to explore how legal discourse and practice allow us to *think* the contemporary political context of Native North America and its conditions of possibility. What can a critical engagement with some of the more abstract and symbolic aspects of law reveal about the concrete and material lives of indigenous peoples living in this historical moment?

LAW

Arguably, no other group has a more confounding relationship to European-settler legal institutions than North American indigenous peoples (Canby 1998; see also Carrillo 1998; Culhane 1998; Harring 1998; Wilkins 1997; Wilkins and Lomawaima 2001). Historically, Euro-settler systems of law developed in part as a response to settler encounters with indigenous populations. Particularly in the Western part of the United States and Canada, law was central to colonizing projects, both in terms of exercising control over indigenous populations and in the creation of national settler identities.[3] Yet the colonial legacies of law are more than strictly "legal"—they exceed the boundaries of legal institutions and are key discursive elements in social and political life in settler states like the United States and Canada. Indigeneity and law are thus inextricably linked.

As Susan Staiger Gooding and Eve Darian-Smith assert, "Writing about law in Native North America requires reading dominant legal regimes themselves as always already constituted in the relation between diverse local, national, international legal and political discourses . . ." (2001:1). A central part of this project is to direct attention to how the historic contours of settler-indigenous encounters became enshrined and encoded in statutes, legal policies, and court decisions, and to further examine how these historic contours shape and intersect with contemporary struggles over identity, political and economic recognition, and self-determination.

Although indigenous peoples have been making claims in North American settler courts since the establishment of those courts, there has been a flurry of legal activity on the part of indigenous groups since the 1960s for various reasons. These include the legacy of the civil rights movement in the US, the formalization of indigenous and multicultural policies in Canada, and the increasing numbers of indigenous peoples participating in mainstream legal systems as practitioners. As a result, "the interpellation of political into legal questions" has become one of the primary ways in which indigenous peoples make political claims in a postcolonial era, especially in Anglo settler states (Dirlik 2001:182). It is this "interpellation" that I am interested in tracking in its contemporary forms, and each of the four case studies provides insight into these questions.

CULTURE

In settler states in the latter part of the twentieth century, a new form of postcolonial reckoning emerged, often embodied in the idioms of culture, difference, and indigeneity. Culture, traditionally thought to be the purview of anthropologists, came to matter in a profound sense in social, political, and legal worlds. As typified by Charles Taylor's now-classic essay "The Politics of Recognition," the recognition of cultural difference was itself broadly considered to be a social and political good. While the dimensions of recognition varied greatly, the law itself was configured as a key site of intervention for what Taylor called "the politics of difference," wherein "what we are asked to recognise is the unique identity of this individual or group, its distinctiveness from everybody else" (1994; see also Gutmann 1994).

In postcolonial democracies such as the US and Canada, nation-states which consider themselves to be culturally and legally plural, issues of cultural difference circulate in multiple spheres and permeate many institutional fields including education, medicine, and in particular, law. The espousal of tolerance and respect for difference has become an important value, one that is expressed both in political and moral terms. As Taylor argues, the failure of liberal nation-states to recognize the differences among their plural citizenry has not only political dimensions, but ethical ones as well. Taylor posits that such a failure can be psychologically damaging to minority groups. In such a conception, *difference* takes on an almost sacred character and becomes a compelling idiom for articulating rights, values, and identities.

The inevitable conflicts and contradictions that emerge as part of discourses of difference push the boundaries of tolerance and respect, and are often described as threatening to a national culture.[4] Scholars Jill Norgren and Serena Nanda describe this tension in the US context as existing between "the need to create national institutions, including law, which unify culturally different groups, and . . . the need to protect human rights by allowing some degree of religious, personal, cultural and local political autonomy" (1996:1). Discourse around Canadian multiculturalism often reflects this same tension (Mackey 1999; Macklem 2001). These contexts of pluralism are essential to understand how *indigeneity* functions in North American courts.

During moments when many cultural anthropologists argued to "forget culture," or at the very least, argued its limits, the "culture concept" began to have significant import in communities and contexts outside of anthropology and outside of academia (see e.g., Brightman 1996; Clifford 1988). Cultural relativism, most simply the idea that cultures have their own internal logic and should be understood and evaluated by these internal rules and not by foreign moral or evolutionary schemes, has been one of cultural anthropology's most influential concepts. Particular conceptions of the cultural, especially the idea of culture and tradition as bounded and static entities, became passé within anthropology just as indigenous peoples were making claims to culture with particular political force. Anthropologist John Cove, among others, has argued that cultural relativism "has provided indigenous peoples in a number of countries with a basis for political action—a factor that has global import for anthropology" (1999:109).[5]

As assertions of traditional and cultural rights have become increasingly important for indigenous peoples throughout the world, these assertions have been critiqued, particularly within certain branches of the academy, as simplistic, essentializing, and incomplete. Debates about what constitutes "culture" or, more specifically, "*a* culture," have been prevalent within the Americanist tradition of anthropology (Darnell and Valentine 1999). Anthropologists have become increasingly uncomfortable with "culture talk" and what they see as "the essentialism, primordialism and primitivism, as well as the residual colonialism" inhering in conceptions of indigenous identity (Guenther 2006:17).[6] This discomfort, however, does not necessarily extend beyond academia, and institutions such as courts have become increasingly fluent in "culture talk." US and Canadian courts in particular have picked up this highly politicized discourse and have begun a process of legal interpretation that has far-reaching consequences for the indigenous peoples living within (and beyond) their borders. Increasingly, anthropologists and others are exploring the discursive and ideological dimensions of this attention to culture in both political and legal spheres (e.g., Dombrowski 2002; Merry 2000; Miller 2001, 2003b; Povinelli 2002a), and *Indigeneity in the Courtroom* follows this line of inquiry.

Beyond the specific debates about the dimensions of culture within anthropology, it is also the case in settler nations that *culture* has often become an elaborate coding of, or in some cases a crude euphemism for, *race*. Gillian Cowlishaw demonstrates how racialization is a key component of indigeneity and advocates anthropological attention to the "racial borderlands" between settler and indigenous identities (Cowlishaw 2000; see also Biolsi 2001; Darian-Smith 2004; Gooding 1994). Thus, part of tracking indigeneity in the courtroom is making explicit how "the culturalization of race" works in legal spheres (Razack 1998).[7]

INDIGENEITY AND THE PRODUCTION OF DIFFERENCE

This book considers how concepts of indigeneity are being deployed and interpreted in both US and Canadian law, particularly in the context of litigation. Specifically, I ask how indigenous difference, *indigeneity*, is produced in both legal and extra-legal spheres. Rather than having a specific referent (indigenous cultural practice and epistemology), *indigeneity* refers to the idea that the content and meaning of indigenous difference is produced in particular contexts, in response to a variety of social, political, and economic forces. In other words, I am not exploring the nature of cultural difference itself, but rather "the processes of *production* of difference in a world of culturally, socially, and economically interconnected and interdependent spaces" (Gupta and Ferguson 1997:43; emphasis in original).

Anthropologist Kirk Dombrowski urges us "to grasp the specific historicity of indigenism itself," and to examine how indigenous claims "are made and heard differently now than they would have been a few years ago" (2002:1062). In other words, "why does a discourse of indigenism succeed now where it failed in the past" (Dombrowski 2002:1062)? In addition to charting the successes of indigeneity in legal contexts, one of the fundamental tensions explored in this book is the contradictory nature of this "success" itself. As the cases in this book demonstrate, claims of indigeneity are not made exclusively by nor in the interests of indigenous peoples.

Law and legal cases provide a necessary framework for exploring and understanding the circulation of ideas and discourse. In this work, I closely examine four recent cases involving indigenous peoples, two from the US and two from Canada. Each chapter can be used as a stand-alone case study, but the chapters themselves may also be read thematically in concert with one another. In Chapter 2, I consider a criminal case in which a Washington state court allowed for the imposition by a traditionalist tribal court of a sentence of banishment for two Tlingit youths convicted of a violent assault. I discuss how the problems surrounding this case were narrated in terms of indigeneity and demonstrate how the deployment of such culturalist discourse in law creates a specific interpretive context in which broader political assertions, especially those concerning sovereignty and land rights, are potentially undermined.

In Chapter 3, I contemplate the use of an indigenous healing circle for a white Catholic bishop accused of sexually assaulting young indigenous women in British Columbia. I explore the process of "erasing indigeneity" in these legal contexts and argue that it is in fact an erasure of entire histories of colonization and their consequences. I argue that it is precisely the erasure of indigeneity in the mainstream courts that allows the healing circle, a place wherein indigeneity is ostensibly celebrated, to take place at all.

In Chapter 4, I look at a recent civil case involving the value of leased Indian land in the city of Vancouver. I explore how the value of indigenous property is constituted through a variety of discursive and material practices that reinscribe colonial property relations and help maintain settler access to Indian lands

Finally, in Chapter 5, I examine the litigation surrounding the remains of Kennewick Man. I trace what I call *genetic indigeneity* as a marker of a discursive shift from a public, scientific, and legal understanding of indigeneity whose predominant metaphor is blood to one in which the predominant metaphor is genes. In the Kennewick Man decisions, the genetic becomes the proving ground of indigeneity and articulates with ideas of racial and morphological difference. I ask what it means that human remains thought to be at least nine thousand years old, and thus clearly "pre-Columbian," do not legally qualify as "Native American" in US courts.

In each of these cases, legal actors deploy the idiom of indigeneity in novel and sometimes unexpected ways. However, I want to suggest that despite their superficial novelty, these cases are not especially anomalous; they are in fact part of continuing processes which rely on reductive pluralist discourses of indigeneity to continue to manage and even deny the existence of a colonial past and a postcolonial present. In terms of substantive content these cases may seem, on the surface at least, not to have much in common with one another beyond the involvement of indigenous peoples in legal disputes. Yet, their juxtaposition allows for an exploration of how indigenous difference is materialized (or erased) in these legal frameworks and how the production of indigeneity itself in these different contexts is a key legal process. Tracking indigeneity in the courtroom—when it is explicitly present and when it is tacitly absent, when it functions as a catalyst in motivating legal claims and decision-making and when it does not—reveals how at the end of the twentieth century law, culture, and difference mutually constitute one another.

2 Banishment

Indigenous Justice and Indigenous Difference in *Washington v. Roberts and Guthrie*

Last Thursday marked the first day of what is without question the most widely publicized legal proceeding in Tlingit history. In the 750-person lumber and fishing town of Klawock, Alaska, 12 self-proclaimed tribal judges pondered the fate of two young criminals. The "tribal court" had the trappings of authenticity: the hall had been ritually purified with a "devil's club" branch, and some of the judges wore red and black ceremonial blankets and gestured with eagle and raven feathers. But there were abundant reasons for skepticism, both of the tribunal and the sentence it was likely to mete out. Not least of which was its presiding magistrate: one of the more creative cross-cultural jurists in recent legal history, Rudy James [Van Biema 1994].

INTRODUCTION

In the mid-1990s, what I term "the banishment case" excited anthropologists, criminologists, indigenous rights activists and others working in the fields of law and justice. In August 1994, Washington State Superior Court Judge James Allendoerfer agreed to a "unique experiment in cross-cultural justice" when he allowed two Tlingit youths convicted in a brutal beating and robbery to delay their mandatory jail sentences and face a traditionalist tribal court in Alaska. With the state court's sanction, the Kuye di' Kuiu Kwaan tribal court banished the two youths, Simon Roberts and Adrian Guthrie, both seventeen at the time, to remote and uninhabited islands in Southeastern Alaska for a period of twelve to eighteen months. According to tribal court organizers and other proponents, the banishment was meant to provide a culturally-specific, therapeutic alternative to incarceration.

Allendoerfer's experiment attracted national and international attention and initiated widespread debates about the potential role that indigenous cultural difference should play in mainstream US jurisprudence. These debates largely centered on the extent to which indigenous cultural traditions and epistemologies should (or could) be accommodated by US legal systems. The banishment also generated a great deal of optimism about the potential of tribal law to revive cultural traditions and to offer positive judicial alternatives for American Indians facing high rates of incarceration.[1] Yet, by the time the banishment ended in late 1995, it was surrounded by controversy and, by most accounts, believed to be a definitive failure.[2] The traditionalist tribal court that arranged the banishment was accused of mismanaging it. There was dissension within various Tlingit communities as to who could legitimately represent their issues in the state court, who could participate in the tribal court, and even whether banishment was a genuine and culturally authentic form of punishment. Further, many at the time expressed concern about the negative impact the banishment case might have on the future of other tribal justice initiatives, and critics have more recently argued that the banishment has worked to discredit the idea of tribal justice in the eyes of the non-Indian public (e.g., Bradford 2000).

But why was the banishment such a failure? According to mainstream accounts in newspapers and magazines, internal tensions between traditionalist tribal bodies and federally-recognized tribal organizations undermined the legitimacy of the process. Further, the credibility of Rudy James, the driving force behind the Kuye di' Kuiu Kwaan tribal court, was consistently challenged throughout the banishment. Many questioned both his motives and his authority, and charges of nepotism, opportunism, and corruption were leveled against James and his supporters. Thus, one might conclude that the banishment's failure was merely a case of individual corruption and of "in-fighting" within a small community.[3]

In this chapter, I explore the colonial and neo-colonial relationships that underlie the production of indigenous difference in the banishment case. I argue that the concept, execution, and ultimate collapse of the banishment is illustrative of a double bind in the cultural production of indigeneity in which the very conditions that enable indigenous peoples to make compelling legal claims based on *difference* can simultaneously lead those claims to failure. I will show how the problems surrounding this case were narrated in terms of indigeneity and demonstrate how the deployment of such culturalist discourse in law creates a specific interpretive context in which broader political assertions, especially those concerning sovereignty and land rights, are potentially undermined.

INDIGENOUS JUSTICE IN NATIVE NORTH AMERICA

Early legal anthropologists looked at different forms of social interaction in order to excavate and articulate the legitimate "rules" of so-called primitive societies (e.g., Bohannan 1957; Gluckman 1955; Llewellyn and Hoebel 1941; Pospisil 1958). They described these rules as "customary law" and as part of discrete, homogeneous, and relatively static communities and paid little or no attention to outside historical forces or power relations. By the 1960s and 1970s, the focus of legal anthropology began to shift away from this "rule-centered paradigm" to a processualist one that understood law as diachronic and as inextricably linked to wider historical, political, social and economic systems including colonialism (Comaroff and Roberts 1981; Moore 1978; Nader and Todd Jr. 1978). Later studies insisted that so-called customary laws were not simply ancient indigenous practices, but rather constructs of colonial governments, initially created as forms of domination and control, and rooted in the complex historical, political, and economic relationships of colonial projects (Chanock 1985; Cohn 1989; Hobsbawm and Ranger 1983; Moore 1986; Snyder 1981). More recent works have made more explicit law's relationship to power, especially in the postcolonial context (see e.g., Garth and Sarat 1998; Hirsch 1998; Keesing 1992; Lazarus-Black 1994; Lazarus-Black and Hirsch 1994; Merry 2000; Nader 1990; 2002; Starr and Collier 1989). Within legal anthropology and other sociolegal disciplines, there has been a great deal of interest in the postcolonial manifestations of indigenous law and custom throughout the world (e.g., Collier 1999; Merry 2000; Miller 2001; Sierra 1995, 2005). Such works have shifted their focus away from more descriptive modes to analyses of how concepts of indigenous culture, tradition, and difference function in complex and often deeply politicized ways.

As indigenous peoples throughout the world continue to assert self-determination and to make claims to territory, intellectual property, artifacts and human remains, and as more nation-states begin to formally recognize indigenous peoples as having certain rights within their systems of law, ethnographic research becomes invaluable in its ability to elucidate subtle forms of local knowledge and to make sense of these forms in larger contexts.

Many claims made by indigenous communities in Canada and the United States have coalesced around issues of law and justice including the implementation of restorative justice. While restorative justice is a broad term encompassing diverse ideas and activities, it is generally understood as an alternative system of justice concerned with restoring balance and harmony to a community damaged by criminal or anti-social activity (Braithwaite 2002; Cragg 1992; Galaway and Hudson 1996; Strang and Braithwaite 2000; Zehr and Toews 2004).[4] Proponents of restorative justice define it in opposition to mainstream or "retributive" justice systems that only seek to punish, arguing that restorative justice is focused on healing all parties affected by crime, namely the victim, the offender and the community (Consedine 1999; Hazlehurst 1994; 1995b; LeResche 1993; Linden and Clairmont 1998).

Although not limited to them, restorative justice has become a guiding principle for many indigenous groups seeking to gain control over the administration of justice in their communities (Dickson-Gilmore and La Prairie 2005; Gray-Kanatiiosh and Lauderdale 2006). In this context, indigenous restorative justice is seen as a strategy of decolonization, as a return to earlier principles and forms of justice that existed in communities prior to the imposition of foreign laws and practices by colonial governments (Hazlehurst 1995a; Lujan and Adams 2004; Porter 1997; Zion 2006). Encompassing a variety of practices including tribal law, peacemaking, and customary law, the realm of indigenous justice is considered to be epistemologically distinct from (and often diametrically opposed to) Western legal formations. While there are subtle variations in the nature of these distinctions, some of the more consistent assertions are that indigenous justice is based on traditional egalitarian principles, and that it works by consensus to restore harmony and heal the community. Many advocates view it as an articulation of community healing, cultural revitalization, and self-determination in response to the ineffective, culturally insensitive, and discriminatory criminal justice systems of the state (Hylton 1995; Lee 1997; Melton 1995; Ross 1996; Ryan 1995; Valencia-Weber 1994; Yazzie 1998; Zion 1998; Zion and Yazzie 1997).

Despite its implied critique of statist justice systems, restorative justice has also become an important alternative for nation-states grappling with the expense of courtroom procedures, ever-expanding rates of incarceration, and public perceptions of a failed system. As a result, governments and courts have been more willing to consider restorative justice measures whether formally or informally.[5] Formalized restorative justice measures, often adapted to be "culturally specific" for indigenous peoples, include mediation, alternative dispute resolution (ADR), diversion programs, and family group conferencing (FGC), all of which look for alternatives to traditional courtroom procedures and incarceration (e.g., Haberfeld and Townsend 1993; Huber 1993; O'Donnell 1995).

Restorative justice has become a highly politicized field, especially in indigenous communities. In both the United States and Canada, indigenous peoples comprise a much larger percentage of the prison population than the general population and are also more likely to be the victims of crime (Greenfeld and Smith 1999; Monture-Angus 1996). Critics of restorative justice in its current forms have argued that measures like family group conferencing, created and sanctioned by the state, are mere "indigenizations" of extant bureaucracies that are firmly rooted in colonial structures and fail to relinquish any real power to indigenous groups (Cunneen 1998; Fleras 1996; Havemann 1988; Tauri 1998; 1999). Other scholars critique the ideological dimensions of restorative justice, asserting that it rests on oversimplified and stereotypical notions of cultural difference with no attention to cultural specificity, histories of religious and political colonization, and anthropological contextualization. They argue that counter-posing typologies of western versus indigenous justice is a part of "continuing colonization," as it fails to address the complexity of these issues (LaRocque 1997:87). Further, the formal nature of state-sanctioned restorative justice programs is often considered to run counter to indigenous cultural conceptions of justice (Guest 1999; Hylton 1995; Nielsen 1991). Yet others suggest that while state law has historically co-opted customary law for its own coercive purposes, it is possible for laws based on indigenous ideas to be counter-hegemonic (e.g., Matsuda 1988; McNamara 1995).

Despite academic critiques of the colonial invention of tradition, arguments advocating a "return" to a pre-contact epistemology and practice in the realm of indigenous justice have great moral and political force.[6] Some scholars have argued that contemporary invocations of "customary law" are not mere descriptions of practice but are also strategic political assertions used to further the claims of indigenous peoples (see e.g., Comaroff 1995; Jackson 1995; Sierra 1995). Others have demonstrated that state institutions and practices constrain indigenous peoples, compelling them to define themselves in the very terms imposed by European colonialism, including contemporary forms of multiculturalism. Specifically, the importance of missionization and other forms of religious colonization in the constitution of discourses about "harmony" and "healing" go unexamined (Comaroff and Comaroff 1991; Nader 1990; Ramos 1998). Further, restorative justice discourses about "traditional" legal practices often rely on these same ethnographic sources and notions of culture from early legal anthropologists.

The banishment was part of an emergent trend among indigenous peoples internationally, but especially in postcolonial Anglo democracies like the US, Canada, Australia and New Zealand, to reclaim customary or tribal law and to make assertions of self-determination through particular cultural-legal claims and practices. For instance, throughout the late 1980s and into the 1990s, some indigenous groups began to assert jurisdiction over their members in criminal sentencing, arguing both that the postcolonial nation-state had failed in its mandate to provide equal and effective justice for all, and that it had an obligation to recognize the legal autonomy of indigenous peoples. Such trends marked a specific shift in indigenous peoples' legal engagements with the state, from mainly seeking redress through statist legal institutions to asserting greater legal autonomy in national and international frameworks. Further, these indigenous assertions operated as powerful critiques that underscored key fictions operating in western legal systems such as colorblind equality and highlighted the social, cultural, and historical specificity of concepts like rights, justice, punishment, and evidence.

At the time of the banishment, there seemed to be great hope for the power of this type of "legal pluralism" to address weaknesses existing in the mainstream legal system. Mainstream courts in the United States were seen to be in crisis, as part of bloated and overextended bureaucratic systems which offered little or no hope for justice, healing or rehabilitation. Activists, scholars, and a broader public alike began to look to tribal courts and other indigenous justice initiatives for solutions. These solutions were nearly always posited as completely other to mainstream jurisprudence.

In what follows, I argue that the conception of an alternative justice system based on an ostensibly radical *indigenous difference* is seriously

limited by appeals to romanticized notions and by a failure to acknowledge
the historical conditions that shape indigenous/settler relations.

THE BANISHMENT

In August 1993, Simon Roberts and Adrian Guthrie, two sixteen-year old
Tlingit cousins from the small community of Klawock, Alaska, were visit-
ing family in Everett, Washington. After an evening of heavy drinking,
they robbed and viciously beat a twenty-five-year-old pizza delivery-man,
Tim Whittlesey, with a baseball bat, and left him for dead. Although Whittlesey survived the attack, he nevertheless sustained permanent injuries to
his hearing and eyesight. Roberts and Guthrie were quickly picked up by
police for the crime, and in 1994 pleaded guilty to charges of aggravated
robbery in Washington State Superior Court. Both faced mandatory prison
sentences of between three and five and a half years.[7]

By the time of their sentencing hearing, Roberts and Guthrie had spent
nearly a year in detention. In response to a petition from Rudy James, a
tribal court judge from the traditionalist Kuye di' Kuiu Kwaan court in
Klawock, Alaska, Judge Allendoerfer agreed to delay the teens' prison sentences and release the young men into James' custody to face a different
kind of sentencing. The youths would be punished by what James claimed
was a traditional Tlingit sentence: banishment.[8] Controversy from different
sources erupted before the custody transfer even took place. The assistant
deputy criminal prosecutor for Snohomish County, Michael Magee, presented a motion in late July of 1994, asking that Allendoerfer reconsider
his decision. Magee asserted, "It seems in reality the defendants are simply
being released to their respective grandparents for the next 18 months, and
the court would be without jurisdiction to direct the grandparents...." He
also pointed out that Rudy James' authority as a tribal judge was disputed
by the Klawock Cooperative Association (KCA)--the only Tlingit tribal
entity recognized by the federal government's Bureau of Indian Affairs
(BIA). Further, according to Magee, the banishment plan was also challenged by another tribal body, the Tlingit-Haida Central Conference, a
tribal court association also recognized by the BIA. The state of Alaska
also opposed the plan, arguing that banishment of a minor "could constitute criminal non-support under the law." Finally, Magee expressed concern about the lack of availability of Tlingit-owned islands appropriate for
the banishment, contending that "'banishment to an island' is not possible
as circumstances now stand."[9]

In response to Magee's motion, Allendoerfer presented a list of ten questions about the banishment plan to defense attorneys and gave them two
weeks to answer. Allendoerfer asked for assurances that the tribal court
proposed by Rudy James actually existed, and that banishment and restitution were in fact Tlingit traditions.[10] Among the questions the judge

asked were a definition of "community" willing to stand behind Guthrie and Roberts, more information about the legitimacy of the tribal court, a determination as to whether government permission was needed for the use of federally-owned lands, and more detail on the plan for restitution.[11]

Around this time, Allendoerfer also received a letter from the KCA, which initially opposed the banishment plan, clarifying its position. KCA president Roseann Demmert wrote that while the association council "agreed in principle" with the Klawock elders' support for holding a combined tribal court, "Unfortunately we are unable to take a formal position of support at this time due to a verbal warning from the Bureau of Indian Affairs of possible negative consequences toward our membership."[12] The newspaper report stated Demmert did not say who made the threat or what the threat entailed. Demmert later said she did not like "what may happen to the boys in prison...but worries about them being placed on an island and whether they will survive."[13]

Despite these early concerns, Allendoerfer signed the release order on August 24, 1994, granting custody of Roberts and Guthrie to Rudy James with the understanding that they would be tried and sentenced by the tribal court. Certain conditions applied including no involvement with drugs, alcohol, or firearms; Allendoerfer warned that if any of the conditions were violated, the teens immediately would return to his court for conventional sentencing. In addition, the tribe promised to post a $25,000 property bond to the court.[14] As part of the arrangement with the state court, Diana Wynne-James, a tribal social worker and Rudy James' wife, was required to write a report to Allendoerfer every three months.[15]

Prosecutors continued to vehemently oppose the arrangement. Chief Deputy Prosecutor Jim Townsend vowed to petition for an appellate review. In a news report, he stated, "We consider it [the banishment] illegal, improper, unconstitutional and wasteful of taxpayer resources. We firmly believe the criminal justice system should try to eliminate racial and ethnic bias and not build it into the system."[16]

While the custody transfer was going ahead, the mainstream press reported on Rudy James' questionable credibility. According to a *Dateline NBC* report broadcast the day after Allendoerfer's ruling, James had nine outstanding civil judgments against him totaling around $60,000. Those judgments included approximately $10,000 in back child support for James' sixteen-year-old son. A *Tacoma News Tribune* report stated that Allendoerfer was aware of James' debts; James was quoted as saying, "I do owe that $60,000, there's no question about that. I don't know anybody who doesn't owe somebody money. . . . I'm ashamed of it, and I'm attempting to pay it back." According to the same report, James had earlier denied to an NBC reporter even knowing the people who had sued him and won judgments; he "then stormed away from the correspondent, calling him a 'queer.'"[17]

The press reported on further credibility problems with James involving allegations of nepotism and conflicts of interest. Five of Rudy James' brothers were judges on the Kuye di' Kuiu Kwaan tribal court, a fact that James relayed to Judge Allendoerfer in Superior Court.[18] Presented by the mainstream press as an impenetrable family unit and an impediment to justice, the tribal court was also seen as a problem by some from within the Klawock community. In the documentary film, *The Eagle and the Raven*, one irate Klawock resident lists other community members who oppose the Kuye di' Kuiu Kwaan tribal court and the banishment because "everyone" knows you can only have one family member on the tribal court (Amiotte 1996).

An even more damaging allegation was that Rudy James' brother Daryle, who had served time on a rape charge, was listed on court documents as a tribal judge. Rudy James denied that Daryle was ever a tribal judge and disavowed any knowledge of how his name got on court documents. James added that the adverse publicity would not deter him: "The tribal court will go on. I'm not going to let a little wind blowing against me stop me."[19]

Despite the controversy, the tribal court proceedings and the banishment had the initial support of the victim's family. An uncle of Tim Whittlesey said that it was enough for the family that Judge Allendoerfer was convinced of the tribal court's legitimacy, saying "It's not an off-the-wall scenario."[20] Max Whittlesey, Tim's father, said the family had accepted the tribe's offer to have community members build a duplex in Everett for Tim and his wife Tonya. He said of the tribal court, "I think we saw the beginning of healing of families on both sides. Rehabilitation is a long process. Time will tell for all three of the young men involved, Tim included."[21]

On September 1, 1994, the Kuye di' Kuiu Kwaan tribal court convened in Klawock. Seventy-five people attended the hearing including the victim Tim Whittlesey and some members of his family. The tribal court proceedings came under the scrutiny of the world. The press was curious about the process, especially focusing on how the court fit into ideas about "native" or "tribal" justice. Note especially the emphasis on tradition, ceremony, and ritual in the following *Associated Press* newspaper report:

> No one was allowed into the hall until it had been ritually cleansed with branches of devil's club, a thorny plant native to the region. Everyone entering the room submitted to purification by being brushed with a cedar bough and wiping their feet at the door. Guthrie and Roberts entered the room through an "entrance of shame," wearing their tribal regalia turned inside out. Each boy was allowed to speak and had a tribal advocate at his side.[22]

According to the same report, elders asked questions about the man who Guthrie and Roberts claimed suggested the robbery, and about the pizza (the toppings, who ate it, its size). [23] The reports also said that some of the questions "elicited smirks from the defendants." When Rudy James expressed disbelief that the crime was done without planning, Guthrie said,

"We didn't sit down and draw a map. . . . I mean, it doesn't take a lot of skill to rob a pizza man."[24]

The twelve elders deliberated for three and a half hours after two days of hearings and ultimately banished the Guthrie and Roberts to separate islands in the Alaskan archipelago for a year to eighteen months. To ensure their safety during the banishment, the youths were to be trained in hunting, given plenty of provisions, and to be checked on regularly by tribal elders. After the sentence was passed, Rudy James said to reporters, "This is not a punishment of a punitive nature. This is not a punishment of endurance to survive in very harsh conditions. It is the judgment of the court that the aim of the sentence is for rehabilitation."[25]

Guthrie and Roberts were supposed to leave immediately after the court, but they spent another two days in Klawock while tribal elders gathered provisions for the banishment. According to reporter Brian Akre, the boys were "lounging in the sun" and one listened to a Walkman as two tribal guards stood watch while waiting to be taken to the islands.[26] While this cynical tone was prevalent in the mainstream media, some people argued that the Tlingit system be given a chance, especially considering the corrupt and dysfunctional justice system of American law. As an editorial in the *Tacoma News Tribune* stated, "If banishment does work in their case, the only complaint will be that there aren't enough cold, lonely islands in the North Pacific to accommodate all of America's violent punks, regardless or race, creed, color or tribe."[27]

Tribal officials would not announce which islands had been chosen for the banishment nor would they reveal their general location and who owned them. Most of the region's one thousand islands officially belong to Tongass National Forest, thus falling under the jurisdiction of the US Forest Service. Forest ranger Greg Griffith said he told tribal officials that a special-use permit was needed in order to allow the boys to stay on federal land. Griffith further doubted one would be granted, and stated, "[Banishment is] not a function of the national forest. It's certainly without precedent on a national forest. We've suggested to them [tribal officials] that there are more appropriate lands on which to carry out this sentence."[28] These statements foreshadowed the conflict that was to come. It was later suggested that the banishment locations were strategically chosen by tribal officials in order to strengthen Tlingit claims to the land. The islands chosen technically fell under the jurisdiction of the US Forest Service, but their tenure was challenged by the Tlingit.

Even after the teens began their banishment, the tribal court continued to have credibility problems. On September 28, 1994, the KCA voted overwhelmingly not to recognize the Kuye di' Kuiu Kwaan Tribal Court. The Vice President of the association said in a telephone interview, "All we're trying to do is straighten up the big mess created by this court." He asserted that members of a tribal court are supposed to be selected by the heads of families in a village, and that Rudy James and his court "were pretty much self-appointed."[29]

By mid-November, however, Diana Wynne James reported to the court that the banishment seemed to be working. She wrote, "There is now an element of sincere sorrow evident in the outlook and demeanor of both youth."[30] She reported that the youths were living in one-room cabins heated with wood. Guthrie and Roberts each had a shotgun, ax, pitchfork, knife, and other basic tools.[31] They ate wild foods supplemented by dried fish and canned food. Both described a feeling of peace and calm, and said they felt they had changed. Roberts, however, received an unauthorized family visit in October. According to Wynne James, "[t]he tribal court gave warning that any other unauthorized visits would be subject to prosecution for interfering with the banishment process."[32]

During March and April of 1995, the US Forest Service noted several news reports that claimed the boys were occupying Forest Service lands. In early April, Snohomish County deputy prosecutor, Seth Fine, filed a motion to have Guthrie and Roberts returned because they had violated the terms of their punishment by living on government land and possessing guns.[33] Tribal judge Byron Skinna responded that Allendoerfer had allowed the teens to possess rifles so they could hunt.

More importantly, however, Skinna claimed that the federal land in question belonged to the Tlingit people "who owned it before the government purchased it," explicitly raising the issue of Tlingit land claims as part of the banishment. In response, prosecutor Fine accused the tribal court of simply pushing its own agenda, stating that the "real problem is that the people who are supposed to be supervising (the teens) have ordered them to break the law." Rudy James denied that any laws had been violated, asserting that "[u]ndisputed and unchallenged, under tribal history, law, custom, culture and tradition, the banishment sites have always been the lands of the [Tlingit]." He then urged prosecutors or other government officials "to produce a valid bill of sale and title to Tlingit lands, waters and resources," challenging the federal government's legitimacy to, and jurisdiction over, the banishment lands in the process.[34]

Tribal attorney Stephen Karl Kortemeier argued that it would thus be Fine's burden to prove why the banishment sites did not belong to the tribe; Fine countered it would be the tribe's responsibility to prove why regulations prohibiting habitation of federal land were illegal. According to Fine, "that kind of dispute does not belong in a criminal case. . . . It is not the business of that [Snohomish County state] court to resolve land-use disputes between native tribal entities and the federal government."[35]

If James and other Kuye di' Kuiu Kwaan members hoped for an opportunity to further their land claims in the context of the banishment case, their hopes were quickly quashed. Despite the fact that Allendoerfer ruled against the prosecution's motion, stating that prosecutors had not proved any willful violation of the court's order on the part of the tribal court, he also effectively undermined any political discourse surrounding Indian sovereignty or land claims by using a strictly culturalist discourse. In his ruling, Allendoerfer asserted that "the defendants had been voluntarily relocated out of National Forest lands and no longer possessed firearms," and that this "voluntary compliance is consistent with the theme of cross-cultural cooperation which is an inherent and integral part of this experiment in cross-cultural justice."[36]

The Kuye di' Kuiu Kwaan Tribal Court was dealt a further blow when, in a Separate appeal in May 1995, the Washington state Court of Appeals ruled that Adrian Guthrie and Simon Roberts would still face mandatory prison time for robbery despite Allendoerfer's suggestion that their banishment could lead to reduced sentences.[37] At the time of original sentencing, Allendoerfer told Guthrie and Roberts that he "made no promises" and that the teens would be "back to Square 1" when they returned to the court post-banishment; he nevertheless expressed hope that the Washington legislature might by that time have "modified the court's authority to deviate from the [mandatory] state sentence," allowing a successful banishment to stand in for prison time.[38]

The Court of Appeals ruled that Allendoerfer's position was improper "because an offender's conduct after the crime cannot justify an exception" and "a court may not delay sentencing to see if the law will change." At a later hearing in July 1995, Allendoerfer gave Guthrie and Roberts the option to finish their exile before imposing their mandatory prison sentences, but reiterated that the banishment could not have any impact on sentencing. Allendoerfer said, "I think this experiment has the potential to make a difference, and I'm going to allow it to run its course."[39] Both youths decided at that time to finish the banishment sentence.

By the summer of 1995, however, it was apparent the banishment experiment was deteriorating. Troubling reports were appearing in local newspapers. For instance, the *Tacoma News Tribune* reported the new banishment sites were in very close proximity to Klawock. Guthrie and Roberts were allegedly receiving unauthorized visits from family members, the media was pursuing them, and other Klawock residents were interfering in the banishment process. Adrian Guthrie was spotted in Craig, Alaska taking a test to obtain his driver's license.[40] Simon Roberts was reportedly living on junk food in a messy campsite. Tribal social worker Diana Wynne James wrote in her report to the court: "It appears that the Klawock community has injected itself into the banishment process, contrary to the intent of the Tribal Court, that this has been to the detriment of the youth."[41] Tribal court members were now describing the banishment as a failure. Embert James, tribal court member and brother of Rudy James, said:

> They're not out on their own, they're not by themselves, they're not thinking about things.... At first, when we had them way out by themselves, you could see a definite improvement in those boys. But then their families came in and got their hands on them, and they quit being dependent on themselves.[42]

Guthrie himself expressed the sentiment that the present banishment location was terrible and made the concept of banishment "an embarrassment and a joke."[43]

By August 1995, Judge Allendoerfer's frustration with the banishment process was evident. After learning of repeated transgressions, Allendoerfer called a status hearing with the tribal court. Rudy James admitted there had been a breakdown of control and that there was "no way of getting around that." Allendoerfer blamed James for failing to get support from other tribal leaders to help to maintain the banishment. He told James, "This crisis in your relationship is at the root of many of your problems."[44]

At the end of September, Allendoerfer ordered Guthrie and Roberts back to court. On October 4, he ruled to end the banishment, citing "some flaws which unfortunately threaten its credibility and integrity." Allendoerfer said he wanted to terminate the experiment while it could still end "on a positive note."[45]

Guthrie and Roberts were sent to prison to serve their original sentences. Guthrie was released in August 1996, and has since been in trouble with the law.[46] He has also failed to make restitution payments to Tim Whittlesey.[47] Guthrie told Allendoerfer in June 1997 that after the media scrutiny died down and the people talking about book and movie deals left, "everybody else left, too, and left me holding the $40,000 bag with my cousin still in prison." A Community Corrections Officer, John Balmat Jr., accused Guthrie of having "a 'poor me' attitude" and feeling "very put out that he has. . .to pay restitution." Balmat also noted Guthrie's "profane, interruptive, argumentative and abusive" tone during a July 1997 telephone conversation.[48] Simon Roberts was released in December 1997, and by available accounts seems to have turned his life around while in prison.

RESTORING JUSTICE? REPRESENTATIONS OF INDIGENOUS DIFFERENCE IN JUSTICE DISCOURSE

Throughout the 1980s and 1990s, increasingly pervasive discussions about the seemingly essential differences existing between indigenous and settler societies emerged. These differences were framed as a clash of cultures, and scholars and activists alike argued that these encounters produced conditions of cultural irreconcilability (e.g., Denis 1997; Torres and Milun 1995). These debates tended to look at assertions of incommensurability as potent epistemological challenges to the legitimacy of mainstream law, and there were further attempts to implement these challenges into politically progressive policies. Borrowing heavily from poststructuralism, the academic elements of this discourse have generally been sympathetic to the often difficult and unequal conditions faced by indigenous communities. While assertions of difference can serve as morally forceful critiques, I argue that structural and discursive conditions limit the strength of these assertions, especially those concerning indigeneity. Ironically, the poststructuralist works mentioned above often uncritically accepted assertions of radical indigenous cultural difference, usually in the name of a progressive politics that recognized the rights of indigenous peoples. More recently, concerns about the limitations of what Spivak famously called "strategic essentialism" (1987:205) have emerged, and scholars and activists alike have realized that politically strategic claims can work in ways that are unexpected, and in many cases, are not in any way politically progressive.[49]

In fact, the deployment of concepts of indigenous difference in US law has a long history that has often been anything but progressive. Legal scholar William Canby describes federal Indian law as the "body of law dealing with the status of Indian tribes and their special relationship to the federal government" (1998:1). Arguably the most complex and contradictory body of law in US history, federal Indian law developed on a case by case basis as a response to a variety of colonial encounters between diverse indigenous groups and settler populations. Throughout its history, the shape of federal law and policy towards Indians shifted in line with more general social attitudes about indigenous peoples, vacillating between the idea that "tribes are enduring bodies for which a geographical base would have to be established and more or less protected" and the idea that "tribes are or should be in the process of decline and disappearance" (Canby 1998:10).

Rooted in pervasive ideologies of indigenous inferiority and connected to the larger project of US nation-building, federal Indian law was mainly concerned with acquiring indigenous territory and gaining access to natural resources. But the effects of federal Indian law were not just economic; as Shari Huhndorf argues, settler concepts of indigenous peoples were also central to the constitution of American national identity (2001).[50]

While the emergence of the banishment was represented as novel, the characterization of Indian law as being incommensurably different from mainstream US law has a long history. In fact, the banishment was not the first time that US settler society responded negatively to the idea of indigenous justice. In August of 1881, on the Great Sioux Reservation in Dakota Territory, an American Indian, Crow Dog, shot and killed another Indian man, the BIA-appointed chief, Spotted Tail. In response, the families of both men came up with a settlement "in accordance with tribal law, for six hundred dollars in cash, eight horses, and one blanket" (Harring 1994:1).[51] This decision infuriated government agents and the settler public more generally, and the following year, Crow Dog was tried and convicted in the Dakota territorial court. He was sentenced to death by hanging. In December 1883, the US Supreme Court overturned Crow Dog's conviction, arguing that the right to make legal decisions was a right of inherently sovereign tribes and that the United States had no jurisdiction over crimes committed in "Indian country."[52] The decision stood, but the furor it provoked ultimately lead to the 1885 passage of the *Major Crimes Act* in the United States Congress, extending federal powers over crimes such as murder in Indian Territory.[53]

In another late nineteenth century case, a US federal court made a decision regarding William Tiger, a man belonging to the Creek Nation and convicted in a tribal court of the murder of another Creek man.[54] In the newly created federal court of appeals for the Indian Territory, Mr. Tiger's lawyer filed a writ of *habeas corpus* on his behalf, arguing that the tribal court had not followed proper procedure in his indictment under Creek law. The court's decision in *Ex parte Tiger* was both curious, given the legalistic nature and dominance of white American culture at the time, and important because it recognized, to a limited extent, the autonomy of Creek law within the nascent American nation-state. The court asserted: "If the Creek Nation derived its system of jurisprudence through the common law, there would be much plausibility in this reasoning [the writ of *habeas corpus*]. But they are strangers to the common law. They derive their jurisprudence from *an entirely different source*" (cited in Harring 1994:69; my emphasis). The court's assertion of difference and autonomy for American Indians, as "strangers to the common law," has peculiar resonance for our contemporary context, a dimension of the banishment case I explore in the following section.

FROM CROW DOG TO BANISHMENT

Participants in the banishment case, Klawock community members, and other Tlingit tribal law practitioners disagreed about many aspects of the banishment. These disagreements or "crises in leadership" as Allendoerfer called them, illustrate a complex and highly politicized system of relationships that is more generally present in contemporary American Indian issues. In this case, claims to leadership and legitimacy were constituted in different ways. For example, when I interviewed Douglas Luna, then Chief Judge of the Tlingit-Haida Central Council, the BIA-recognized tribal court entity, he was angry with the media's portrayal of a case he believed did not warrant the attention.[55] He challenged Rudy James' legitimacy and credibility, asserting that James had no jurisdiction because he was not a member of a BIA-recognized tribe. Rudy James, however, refers to himself as "ThlauGoo YailthThlee -- The First and Oldest Raven," asserting that he is directly descended from the men who were leaders at the time of European conquest, and that his leadership was foretold in dreams (James 1997). Luna further questioned whether or not Guthrie and Roberts were really "Indians" (i.e. on any tribal membership list).

My argument here is that we cannot simply see this case as a quest for cultural and political recognition on the part of the Tlingit. This simplification effaces the complex set of historical and political relationships that are the legacy of European colonialism in the Americas. For instance, as we have seen in the banishment case, legitimate tribal courts in the United States are those sanctioned by the Bureau of Indian Affairs (BIA), a legacy that has its basis in the Indian Reorganization Act of 1934.[56] As Ward Churchill and Glenn T. Morris argue, the Indian Reorganization Act "was imposed by the United States to supplant traditional forms of indigenous governance in favor of a tribal council structure modeled after corporate boards" (1992:15). An ostensibly democratic process, each American Indian nation was required to hold a referendum. These referenda were manipulated by Commissioner of Indian Affairs, John Collier, and have had long-reaching effects including "a deep division between 'traditionals' and 'progressives' (who endorse the IRA form of government) on many reservations to this day" (Churchill and Morris 1992:15). Thus, any attempt to inscribe the term "Tlingit" or "indigenous" with some kind of strictly culturalist meaning not only ignores historical and political processes that have shaped much of contemporary indigenous social life, but also enables the state to discredit any claims that violate this reified and constructed category. In other words, such terms operate in a context in which political conflicts, like the one exemplified by the clash between James and Luna, are inevitable; dominant culture, as represented by Allendoerfer's court and the media, then uses those very conflicts to delegitimate the banishment.

American Indians often find themselves in the paradoxical position of having to rely on the imprimatur of the US government to *recognize* their *pre-existing* sovereignty and rights. As Torres and Milun point out in their discussion of the Mashpee, the legal and political history of indigenous peoples predictably results in these kinds of paradoxical and conflicting situations with the government:

> The politics of historical domination reduced the Mashpee to having to petition their "guardian" to allow them to exist, and the history of that domination has determined in large measure the ways the Mashpee must structure their petitions. The conflict between these systems of meaning - that of the Mashpee and that of the state - is really the question of how we can "know" which history is most "true" (1995:49).

This type of conflict is present is the banishment case. For instance, a contradiction inheres in the American Indian claim to inherent self-government or always-existing sovereignty. Rhetorically, this stance is imperative to begin legally to declare sovereign status; it must not be seen as a request for status, but a demand for recognition of something already extant. Nonetheless, American Indian sovereignty within the contemporary American context remains an issue of negotiation. In which forms will a limited sovereignty be allowed by the US government?

As sociolegal scholars have long argued, it is crucial that we look at a broader political and cultural context to understand the operation of the law. Within the context of this case where "tribal culture" and issues of its legitimacy and authenticity are of the utmost importance, this strategy demonstrates how many different sites are engaged in such an issue. For instance, the type of deferred sentencing used in the banishment has been legally possible for some time, so why and how did it come to be employed at this particular moment? [57] To argue that the potentiality for such an unprecedented sentence lay solely within the law itself is counterintuitive. Other factors must have contributed. For example, a widespread disillusionment with American jurisprudence engendered the search for alternatives. In the banishment case, editorials often pointed to the sorry state of crime and punishment in the US, arguing it was time to try something new: "His [Allendoerfer's] action shows a respect for the tribe's cultural approach to punishment, and if it results in restitution--something all too absent from mainstream justice--all the better."[58]

The banishment case itself can be understood both as an assertion of sovereignty, and a struggle for recognition from a wider public. The negotiations between the Kuye di' Kuiu Kwaan tribal court and the Washington state criminal justice system exemplify, on the one hand, the seemingly irreconcilable positions occupied by the players involved, and, on the other, the consistent bargaining over the extent to which sovereignty will be allowed. For instance, the need rhetorically to assert sovereignty (as something inherent and pre-nation-state) is directly opposed to Congress' position of plenary power. Each stance recognizes that tribes are, in some form, governments, but the operating definitions of "governments" in this instance are radically different: full sovereign with jurisdiction over land and people versus domestic dependent nation. The Department of Justice, in its vague policies, has no intention of fully turning over jurisdiction to American Indian tribes; instead, it wishes to find a complementary system, integrating Western and tribal law, but nonetheless maintaining its status as guardian.

Prosecutors and others in the public framed the banishment case in such a way as to preclude any discussion about sovereignty. They argued instead that the real issue was the introduction of a "competing system" that challenged the authority of American law on the basis of race and minority status. Attempts to delegitimize the banishment process often fell into the rhetoric of the unfairness of differential treatment, asserting the law's objectivity and color-blindness. It was also the contention of the prosecution that sovereignty claims have no place in a criminal proceeding. Nevertheless, claims to sovereignty did occur within the confines of the criminal justice system: claims over jurisdiction, land tenure, and conceptions of law and justice. The tribal court still operated within the system, but outside of the usual forums (e.g., land claims trials). It is a different way of framing issues both within the court system and for a wider public. The notoriety of the criminal case brought public attention to Tlingit issues in a way land tenure hearings often do not. The tribal court was able to critique the criminal justice system from inside by offering an alternative to it, and by asserting its jurisdiction over Guthrie and Roberts.

What happens to this critique when, by all accounts, the banishment sentence failed? The objectives stated by the Kuye di' Kuiu Kwaan tribal court (i.e. that the boys be rehabilitated and that restitution be paid to the victim) were not entirely met, Allendoerfer ended the experiment in frustration, and as was shown in the preceding section, public reactions to the case were overwhelmingly cynical. The suggestion that Roberts and Guthrie were used to put forth another agenda and were left holding the proverbial bag when that agenda was unsuccessful must certainly be considered. What do such suggestions do to the legitimacy of tribal courts and of American Indian claims more widely?

I want now to return to Allendoerfer's claim that the "crisis in [the] relationship" among members of Tlingit communities was "at the root of many problems" in order to discuss the ultimate failure of the banishment. Allendoerfer's statement reflects a lack of understanding of, or refusal to engage with, the historical emergence and continuing political complexity of tribal courts. Allendoerfer represents his state court as distanced from these "crises," and further, he presents himself as simply a neutral arbiter rather than as a representative of an institution deeply implicated in colonial and neo-colonial relationships. The court posits itself as benevolent pluralist while it treats matters of indigenous difference as issues of cultural sensitivity. It was, however, unprepared to encounter another kind of indigenous difference, one that recognizes the complex and multilayered cultural and political lives of contemporary indigenous communities. Rather, Allendoerfer was looking for a coherent representative/representation of *the* Tlingit community, one lacking the conflict and contradiction so often reflected in so-called modern societies, but considered antithetical to indigenous ones. This, of course, was a need the involved parties were unable to fulfill.

When interviewed about the case in 1994, Judge Allendoerfer told reporters, "I am pleased and proud of what I did. If it turns out well, I will do it again. And again."[59] While it seems likely that Allendoerfer will not be attempting another "cross-cultural experiment" in the near future, what will courts in other parts of the country try and to what effect?

Anthropologist Bruce G. Miller has advocated close attention to what he characterizes as a "dangerous moment" in the North American trend toward the "awkward position of developing programs for the self-administration of justice following a long period of disruption imposed by the state" (2003:136). The danger is not simply that the colonial and postcolonial histories that underlie such initiatives predestine them to failure. Rather, the danger is that the culturalist discourse of indigenous difference will continue to preclude any deep discussion of key issues such as sovereignty, land rights, and the social and material conditions of Native North America.

3 Healing the Bishop

Sexual Violence, Consent, and the Legal Erasure of Colonial History in *R. v. O'Connor*

Bishop May Avoid Trial
A Roman Catholic bishop might be able to avoid a new trial on sex charges, a top B.C. justice official says. Ernie Quantz, the chief prosecutor in the Attorney-General's office, said Wednesday that Bishop Hubert O'Connor and two women complainants are considering an alternative aboriginal healing process. Mr. Quantz told CBC Radio that the Crown may deem it in the public interest not to proceed with the case if the healing process is used. Bishop O'Connor, 71, was the highest Roman Catholic official in Canada ever convicted of a sex crime when he was found guilty in 1996. He was sentenced to 2½ years in prison, but was released on $1,000 bail when he appealed after serving six months. He was cleared of indecent assault by the B.C. Court of Appeal in March [*The Globe and Mail*, 1998].[1]

INTRODUCTION

During the summer of 1998, Hubert O'Connor, a white Catholic bishop and former Indian residential school principal, participated in what a local magazine termed "a centuries-old native ceremony": an indigenous healing circle.[2] Seven years earlier, O'Connor had been indicted on criminal charges for sexual offences he had allegedly committed in the 1960s while principal of the Cariboo Indian Residential School in Williams Lake, British Columbia. Six charges, ranging from rape to indecent assault, were brought on behalf of five indigenous women, all of whom were O'Connor's former students and/or employees. While O'Connor acknowledged having sexual relations with these women, and admitted to fathering a child with one of them, he denied having committed any illegal acts, maintaining that these relationships had been consensual.

In 1996, after two trials and multiple appeals, O'Connor was convicted in a Vancouver provincial court on two of the counts: rape and indecent assault. Yet two years later, in 1998, the British Columbia Court of Appeal (BCCA) overturned these convictions, citing errors by the trial judge, and ordered another trial for only the rape charge [*R. v. O'Connor* (24 March 1998), Vancouver CA022299 (BCCA); hereafter *R. v. O'Connor*].

Faced with another trial, O'Connor's defense attorney proposed the healing circle "to try and bring resolution without going any further in the court process."[3] The Crown, under the auspices of the province's attorney-general, accepted the proposal, in part because the last remaining complainant, Marilyn Belleau, and other members of her community agreed to it, and in part because it was unclear whether or not O'Connor would be convicted in a third trial.[4] Organizers also presented the circle as an instance of indigenous restorative justice that would foster an intersection between the cultural traditions of indigenous peoples and mainstream criminal processes. Further, in the context of widespread allegations of rampant physical, sexual, and emotional abuse at church-run Indian residential schools across the province, and of a burgeoning number of lawsuits against participating churches, the circle was presented as an example of "the possibility of healing between individuals and between B.C.'s natives and the Catholic Church."[5] As a result, the first government-sanctioned indigenous healing circle in the province of British Columbia was for Bishop O'Connor.

The province's decision to convene a healing circle for a white bishop accused of sexually assaulting indigenous women infuriated many and provoked a national outcry. Yet the furor focused almost exclusively on the healing circle itself (specifically on the inappropriateness of such a sanction for a white bishop) with virtually no discussion of *how* or *why* the BCCA overturned O'Connor's convictions in the first place. In both public and legal discourse, the courts and the healing circle were consistently treated as separate spheres, and there was a troubling lack of attention paid to how they were connected to each other. The courts were constructed as normative legal spaces while the healing circle was presented as an "alternative" sphere charged, in large part, with the task of addressing the inadequacies of the former.

In this chapter, I shift the discussion of indigenous justice from the United States to Canada and specifically engage some of its gendered dimensions. I look beyond the outrage at the participation of a white bishop accused of sexually assaulting indigenous women in a healing circle. Instead, I examine the production of *indigeneity* in the realm of Canadian law. I challenge the tacit presumption that the courts and the healing circle are discrete and make explicit some of the ways in which these spheres are structurally and discursively interconnected in order to discuss how idioms of indigeneity are functioning in postcolonial courts. By examining both the healing circle *and* the BCCA's decision to overturn O'Connor's conviction in *R. v. O'Connor*, I argue that the culturalist discourse surrounding O'Connor's circle elides the very thing it is supposed to address: namely, the ongoing effects of colonization on indigenous peoples, and on indigenous women in particular. In this configuration of legal spaces, the healing circle is posited as the cultural space of *de-colonization*, thus enabling the mainstream courts to ignore the legacies of colonial history that created the very conditions that brought O'Connor into prolonged contact with the plaintiffs.

HEALING THE BISHOP: INDIGENEITY
AND LEGAL "ALTERNATIVES"

> Aboriginal perspectives on justice are different. That difference is a re-
> flection of distinctive Aboriginal world views and in particular a holis-
> tic understanding of peoples' relationships and responsibilities to each
> other and to their material and spiritual world [Royal Commission on
> Aboriginal Peoples 1996].

> As the nation stretches out its hands to ancient Aboriginal laws (as
> long as they are not "repugnant"), indigenous subjects are called on to
> perform an authentic difference in exchange for the good feelings of
> the nation and the reparative legislation of the state. But this call does
> not simply produce good theater, rather it inspires impossible desires:
> *to be* this impossible object and to transport its ancient prenational
> meanings and practices to the present in *whatever* language and moral
> framework prevails *at the time of enunciation* [Povinelli 2002a:6; em-
> phasis in original].

In this section, I discuss the emergence of indigenous forms of justice in postcolonial Canada, and place O'Connor's healing circle, and his case more
generally, within a particular "time of enunciation"—a time when discourses
of culture and difference are the prevailing language and moral framework
for indigenous peoples in settler Canada. By demonstrating how the healing
circle is constituted as an "indigenous," and thus explicitly *culturalized* space
(Razack 1998), I show how this focus elides a range of factors important for
understanding *R v. O'Connor* in broader perspective.

Because official discourses marked the healing circle as a distinctly
"indigenous" space, the reductive culturalist discourse of indigenous tradition and healing was left virtually unchallenged in mainstream discourse.
Such reified notions of indigeneity are common in the Canadian public
sphere. Especially problematic, however, was that the circle itself was the
only space wherein the complainants were recognized in any sense as *indigenous* legal subjects.

The healing circle was a seven-hour, private ceremony, led by complainants' spokesperson, Charlene Belleau (also Marilyn Belleau's sister-in-law),
and then-assistant deputy attorney-general for BC, Ernie Quantz. Its stated
purpose was to allow the victim and the perpetrator as well as their families and communities to come together to reach an understanding in an
attempt to begin a process of healing and reconciliation. The healing circle
was seen as an example of restorative justice—such a process is supposed
to allow the victim to confront her perpetrator without interruption, something arguably not possible within the confines of conventional courts.
Charlene Belleau asserted the benefits of such a process: "In a circle, there
is no hierarchy; everyone is equal."[6]

There are no public transcripts from the healing circle, only published newspaper reports based mainly on post-ceremony interviews as well as O'Connor's formal public apology. Reporter Barbara McLintock describes the healing circle in the following way:

> In the Hubert O'Connor case, the circle was divided into three parts. In the first and smallest circle, victim Marilyn Belleau confronted O'Connor with her feelings about the wrong he had done, and O'Connor apologized. A total of 38 people participated in the next phase, in which members of the victim's family and native elders also talked about the pain they'd suffered, not just from O'Connor's actions but also from the residential-school system. O'Connor then had a chance to reply and apologized to them. In the final phase, more community members joined the circle to hear formal, written apologies from O'Connor and from Bishop Jerry [sic] Wiesner on behalf of the Roman Catholic Church. The circle then closed with native songs, drumming and prayers.[7]

According to press accounts, the main participants found the circle a gratifying experience. Complainant Marilyn Belleau expressed both her satisfaction with the process and her weariness at "being victimized by the courts": "I chose to participate in this healing circle to empower myself. I was able to confront him [O'Connor] with the hurts and pains he has caused me. I have had to live with this pain for over 30 years."[8]

O'Connor did not speak to the press, but rather communicated through his attorney. Defense lawyer Chris Consadine said the bishop "found [the circle] very, very difficult," but felt more at peace afterwards.[9] Only O'Connor's formal written apology, in which he apologized for his "breach as a priest" and his "unacceptable behavior," was made public. His apology enraged many, especially because he admitted to no criminal behavior; instead, he spoke rather euphemistically about the harm he had caused and his hope that there would "be a healing of the rifts between our communities."[10]

Some of the most trenchant critiques focused on the case's ethical aspects and its potential for setting dangerous legal precedents, especially in cases involving violence against women. Proponents of the use of restorative justice initiatives in indigenous communities throughout the province were concerned about the negative publicity and its possible impact on nascent initiatives.

The Crown's decision not to further pursue O'Connor in the courts and to allow him to participate in the healing circle was controversial. Many felt that O'Connor, as a white priest, was an inappropriate candidate for a culturally-specific indigenous healing circle, and that his alleged violations were far too serious for such an option. Women's groups in particular argued that the decision exemplified the province's ongoing lack of concern for violence against women, especially indigenous women. They argued that O'Connor had not been suitably punished for his violation of Belleau and the other women. While feminist critics were careful to point out that they supported Belleau's and the other complainants' decision to participate in the healing circle, they nevertheless maintained that it was an inappropriate sanction for O'Connor, and that it set a dangerous precedent for future cases involving violence against women.[11]

RESTORATIVE JUSTICE IN CANADA

The 1990s were an especially fruitful time for restorative justice initiatives both in indigenous communities throughout the world and in other non-indigenous contexts including state-sponsored experiments such as Alternative Dispute Resolution (ADR), Family Group Conferencing (FGC), and mediation.[12] Critiques of both the philosophy and practice of mainstream legal systems were appearing with greater frequency not only in academic spheres, but also in the Canadian public. Additionally, a number of high profile public inquiries into Canada's criminal justice system presented damning evidence that indigenous peoples were disproportionately targeted at all levels of the system (Manitoba 1991a; Manitoba 1991b; Royal Commission on Aboriginal Peoples 1996). Particularly relevant for indigenous communities were the high rates of incarceration *and* victimization experienced both by men and women in those communities. As the now famous *Report of the Manitoba Justice Inquiry* asserted in its introduction:

> The justice system has failed Manitoba's Aboriginal people on a massive scale. It has been insensitive and inaccessible, and has arrested and imprisoned Aboriginal people in grossly disproportionate numbers. Aboriginal people who are arrested are more likely than non-Aboriginal people to be denied bail, spend more time in pre-trial detention and spend less time with their lawyers, and, if convicted, are more likely to be incarcerated.
>
> It is not merely that the justice system has failed Aboriginal people; justice also has been denied to them. For more than a century the rights of Aboriginal people have been ignored and eroded. The result of this denial has been injustice of the most profound kind. Poverty and powerlessness have been the Canadian legacy to a people who once governed their own affairs in full self-sufficiency (Manitoba 1991a; Manitoba 1991b).

Such reports made a very clear link between the devastation wrought by colonization and the present conditions of indigenous peoples. Justice was thus identified by both indigenous groups and governmental institutions as an arena for a kind of *de*-colonization, a space of "self-sufficiency" not only for the implementation of practical solutions to the specific injustices endured by indigenous peoples within the criminal justice system, but also for the revitalization of indigenous epistemologies and cultural practices (e.g., Green 1998; Warry 1998). Thus, within this context, concepts of restorative justice were especially current because they offered both a compelling moral critique of the institutions of settler society and an opportunity for indigenous peoples to gain greater powers of self-determination. Throughout the 1990s, federal and provincial governments were especially interested in supporting (both philosophically and, in a limited way, fiscally) certain kinds of "culturally-specific" justice initiatives, and many groups invested their energies and resources into delimiting and defining the nature of "traditional" indigenous justice.[13]

During the time of O'Connor's circle, there was increased interest in using formal restorative justice approaches in sexual assault and domestic violence cases, in part because mainstream approaches were considered to be culturally biased and largely ineffectual (Bellerose 1993; Carbonatto 1995; Murray 1998; O'Donnell 1995; Strang and Braithwaite 2002). Gender violence in indigenous communities in Canada and the US is widespread, a fact many attribute to the violence of colonialism and the resulting denigration of women's status (Fiske 1991; McGillivray and Comaskey 1999; Monture-OKanee 1992; Nahanee 1993; Smith 2005; Stevenson 1999).[14] Yet critiques from indigenous feminist-activists and others questioned whether or not such practices are appropriate for victims of gender violence (Aboriginal Women's Action Network 2001; Balfour 2008; Cameron 2006; Coker 2006; Crnkovich 1995, 1996).[15]

In 1996, the Royal Commission on Aboriginal Peoples (RCAP) released an influential report on Aboriginal justice, entitled *Bridging the Cultural Divide*. The comprehensive report, several hundred pages long, reviews "the historical and contemporary record of Aboriginal people's experience in the criminal justice system to secure a better understanding of what lies behind their over-representation there" (Royal Commission on Aboriginal Peoples 1996:xi). Like the *Manitoba Justice Inquiry*, RCAP affirmed what many indigenous peoples had been consistently asserting for years—that it is impossible to understand the contemporary situations faced by them without making an explicit link to the impact of colonization: "In large measure these problems are themselves the product of historical processes of dispossession and cultural oppression" (ibid.). Yet, despite this initial contextualization, the RCAP report goes on to assert the following in its final recommendations:

> The Canadian criminal justice system has failed the Aboriginal peoples of Canada—First Nations, Inuit and Métis people, on-reserve and off-reserve, urban and rural—in all territorial and governmental jurisdictions. *The principal reason for this crushing failure is the*

fundamentally different world views of Aboriginal and non-Aboriginal people with respect to such elemental issues as the substantive content of justice and the process of achieving justice (Royal Commission on Aboriginal Peoples 1996:309; my emphasis).

Although the report presents a structural understanding of how colonialism has shaped criminal justice institutions and practices in relation to indigenous peoples, the "crushing failure" of these institutions and practices is nevertheless primarily defined as a *cultural* problem, the result of "fundamentally different world views." This conception was reproduced in the context of the healing circle and is thus essential to understanding how indigeneity was produced in this case.

RCAP's explanation appeals to a particular ideal of indigeneity without recognizing the reductive nature of "the fundamentally different world views of Aboriginal and non-Aboriginal people." It also shapes the discourse in such a way as to limit critique. Because this conception of indigeneity is defined primarily in terms of culture, critiques of cases like O'Connor's tend to focus narrowly on cultural concerns while missing the larger forces that structured the situation in the first place and allowed O'Connor's convictions to be overturned.

Bridging the Cultural Divide, while presenting a reasoned critique of colonialism, nevertheless defines its legacy as a problem of cultural insensitivity rather than an ongoing phenomenon with real symbolic and material stakes.[16] In other words, indigenous peoples are forced to articulate their critiques and their desires through a discourse of culture and difference, the prevailing "language and moral framework" in late twentieth century settler Canada. The problem is not only that this language and moral framework is limiting—all discourses, to some extent, are—but also that it serves to elide the very processes that produce it in the first place. In other words, indigenous culture and difference are represented as something outside of the difficult conditions of postcolonial Canada rather than as a construct produced in the context of these very conditions (Povinelli 2002a).

Anthropologist Elizabeth Povinelli further argues that postcolonial nation-states place "an impossible demand" on indigenous peoples to "desire and identify with their cultural traditions in a way that just so happens, in an uncanny convergence of interests, to fit the national and legal imaginary of multiculturalism" (2002a:8). She demonstrates that the process of defining culture in postcolonial contexts is both deeply fraught and politicized, and that this process must be seen as part of broader structural and discursive forces. The specific discourse of indigeneity exemplified in *Bridging the Cultural Divide* not only reflects a more general Canadian multicultural imaginary, one that fits with statist interests, but it also permeates Canadian legal spaces including courts and their "alternatives." As a result, the healing circle is an example of such an impossible demand on indigenous peoples. In O'Connor's case, the discourse of indigeneity profoundly enables and shapes both the healing circle and the mainstream court decisions themselves, albeit in different ways. The healing circle is posited as the pre-modern, pure space in contrast to the morass and excesses of the mainstream legal system. Within this discursive framework, "recognition" of difference is the path to mend "the crushing failure." It enables the courts, for example, to avoid addressing larger structural issues of the residential school experience in evaluating O'Connor's case, and the discourse of "bridging the cultural divide" mobilizes the healing circle as a legitimate option.

Having given a background for the emergence of discourses of culture and difference in the context of indigenous justice in Canada, I want now to return to a discussion of O'Connor's healing circle. Specifically, I examine the constitution of that circle as an explicitly indigenous cultural space as well as the implications of such a constitution. What makes this an "aboriginal healing circle," and how do we recognize it as such? I begin with a brief discussion of the media accounts of the circle. These accounts are coded for their specific 'indigenous' content:

The circle then closed with native songs, drumming and prayers.[17]

Healing circles are a traditional native Indian way of repairing harm to people through dialogue among the affected parties in a carefully controlled and private setting under the leadership of tribal elders.[18]

So with the smell of sacred sage smoke drifting through a native meeting hall in Alkali Lake on Monday, O'Connor apologized to his former students for what he called "my breach as a priest and my unacceptable behaviour, which was totally wrong. I took a vow of chastity and I broke it."[19]

In these accounts, indigeneity is evoked through culturalized objects such as drums and sage, as well as through reductive discourses of sacredness, healing, and tradition. Such descriptions mark the space as indigenous, as outside of settler culture and its legal institutions, and as representative of true difference. The healing circle is a space not only physically removed from the court, but also temporally distanced from it through the invocation of "centuries old" tradition.

Such accounts should not be read as simply culturally sensitive descriptions of indigenous practice, but rather as part of a broader postcolonial settler discourse that struggles to come to terms with its colonial past. For instance, the descriptions of the healing circle must be understood as part of longstanding evolutionary paradigms wherein indigenous peoples were seen to represent earlier (and inferior) stages in human development. At certain historical moments, however, settler societies have inverted these positions, positively valuing aspects of indigenous life and practice (as long as they were not objectionable) as a way "to resolve widespread ambivalence about modernity as well as anxieties about the terrible violence marking the nation's origins" (Huhndorf 2001:2). Even when valued positively, this inversion leaves intact the radical distinction between settler and indigenous, a distinction deeply rooted in colonial practice and ideology.

The press presented the healing circle as a manifestation of the "fundamentally different world views" described in RCAP's report as opposed to a materialization of complex postcolonial conditions. The healing circle itself rests on the presumption that centuries of colonialism can be erased (or, at the very least, mitigated) by the invocation of "authentic" or "pure" culture. In such a context, indigenous culture takes on a kind of mystical quality, one which can magically transform a racist and bankrupt process into a moment of true interpersonal connection. The healing circle becomes a way of "bridging the cultural divide" between indigenous and settler peoples. As one of the newspaper accounts asserted: "The traditional healing circle gives victims, their families and perpetrators the chance to fully express themselves and reach an understanding, with no one being allowed to interrupt the other."[20]

Emma LaRocque calls the deeply problematic constructions of culture which circulate in these discourses, "the misuse of 'traditions,'" distinguishing between oversimplified anthropological or legal constructs and the contemporary lived experience of indigenous peoples (1997). In his discussion of indigenous justice practices among Coast Salish peoples in both Canada and the U.S., anthropologist Bruce G. Miller cautions against the use of "primordialist discourses that uncritically incorporate concepts of healing, restoration, and elderhood without due regard for the relations of power between the various segments of the community" (Miller 2001).[21] Finally, demonstrating that notions of tradition cannot be seen outside of the institutional structures that define and deploy them, Sherene Razack reveals that it "continues to be primarily white male judges and lawyers with little or no knowledge of history or anthropology who interpret Aboriginal culture and its relevance to the court" (1998:72). What all of these scholars point out is that there needs to be a distinction made between the complex cultural lives of contemporary indigenous peoples and the culture concept deployed in the context of settler institutions.

Another place in which the discourse of "bridging the cultural divide" was deployed was in the official discourse of the Roman Catholic Church (RCC). As Gerry Wiesner, then vice-president of the Canadian Conference of Catholic Bishops, said:

> As a Catholic bishop I am ashamed of the violations that were actually committed by Catholic people in a school that taught Catholic values and beliefs. . . . We find wisdom in aboriginal spiritual traditions for restorative justice and reconciliation.[22]

The important question here is *what* it means to "find wisdom in aboriginal spiritual traditions for restorative justice and reconciliation" in the specific context of O'Connor's case and in the broader context of widespread physical, emotional, and sexual abuse in Catholic-run Indian residential schools. In Canada, the RCC has been notoriously reluctant to settle civil residential school claims, and has mounted vigorous defenses for its criminally accused, including O'Connor. In what has come to be called the residential school scandal, RCC organizations are named in nearly 70 percent of the 12,000 lawsuits filed. There has been particular concern about the financial stability of the Church as well as the health of their missionary endeavors. Some religious orders have filed for creditor protection, although the RCC in Canada boasted that its membership had increased despite the sex scandals.[23]

Yet, the RCC's recalcitrant stance toward the settlement of residential school claims seems diametrically opposed to the values of restorative justice and reconciliation evoked in the healing circle. Wiesner's emphasis on healing is not idiosyncratic in the least, but rather is reflected in broader RCC discourse. Discourses of healing and reconciliation are widespread, especially in the context of residential schools, and they are ubiquitous tropes in Catholicism more generally. I contend, then, that these are not in fact opposed at all. I take very seriously Razack's contention that an "emphasis on cultural diversity too often descends, in a multicultural spiral, to a superficial reading of differences that makes power relations invisible and keeps dominant cultural norms in place" (1998:9). The specific marking of the healing circle as an "indigenous" space entails a particular reading of the cultural. Such a reading references imagined precontact or prenational egalitarian traditions, extant prior to colonization, and assumes that their contemporary invocation respatializes the violent relationship between colonizer and colonized. Thus what allows Wiesner and others to simultaneously appreciate "aboriginal spiritual traditions" in the specific context of the healing circle *and* to be part of a body actively resisting the settlement of claims is a particular conception of cultural difference, one that fails to recognize how "power and dominance function through more liberal, inclusionary, pluralistic, multiple and fragmented formulations and practices concerning culture and difference" (Mackey 1999:5). What Razack calls "culture talk" only emerges in reference to the healing circle—it is not referenced in any of the criminal court decisions, and nothing explicitly cultural is used to better understand the events in question.

In the context of restorative justice, there is often a tenuous relationship between what we know of precontact justice practices and contemporary ones. I do not read the tenuousness of this relationship as particularly problematic nor am I challenging the "authenticity" of the healing circle. The focus of my critique is the need for indigenous peoples to perform authenticity in order to make gains in postcolonial, multicultural settler societies (Povinelli 2002a, 2004). The problem is the presumption of, and in some cases the insistence on, direct continuity between the pre- and postcolonial. Also problematic is the notion that all indigenous difference can be distilled into several major traits, ones articulated in opposition to the perceived traits of mainstream or "non-indigenous" justice systems. Such a context occludes the racialized and gendered spatial relationships that bring people into contact in the first place, a context that is absolutely necessary to understand Bishop O'Connor's case. Attention to these historicized aspects of indigeneity by the courts may have produced a very different outcome in *R. v. O'Connor.*

CONSENT IN *R. v. O'CONNOR*

> And so the issue that this court is going to have to come to grips with . . . is whether or not, in the context of the relationship that had developed, whether or not the failure to articulate the lack of consent and whether or not any failure to physically resist in terms of attempting to fight off this man who was considerably larger than any of these complainants at the time, by the way, whether or not in circumstance that can be taken to signify actual consent or perhaps apparent consent, and that's an issue that I anticipate counsel are alive to and the court will be as well [*R. v. O'Connor*].

The legal dimensions of *R v. O'Connor* hinge on issues of consent (or lack thereof). Did the complainants consent to have sexual relations with O'Connor, or did his authority as priest, principal and employer vitiate any genuine consent? Did the complainants sufficiently resist O'Connor's advances? Did they resist at all? Is mere submission adequate to constitute legal consent, or is consent "a matter of the conscious exercise of the will"? (1998:par. 43). And even if there was no genuine consent, did the complainants adequately indicate their objections to O'Connor? In his 1996 ruling at O'Connor's trial, Justice Wally Oppal accepted the Crown's position that while there was "no evidence that the consent was extracted by threats and violence," there nevertheless could be "no genuine consent on the part of the complainants due to their particular circumstances as former students and then employees of the school"(1998:par. 68). Despite the absence of any statutory reference to the vitiation of consent by the exercise of authority at the time of the violations, Oppal contended that there was sufficient precedent in both English and Canadian common law to support the Crown's position. However, in 1998, the British Columbia Court of Appeal accepted the defense's argument, and found that "the trial judge was wrong in concluding that the exercise of authority could vitiate consent under the rape provisions of the Code as they existed at the time of the events in question" (1998:par. 66). As a result, the court asserted that Justice Oppal had not adequately resolved the issue of consent in O'Connor's criminal trial, and it was thus left with no choice but to overturn both convictions, and to order a new trial for only the rape charge. Oppal's decision produced a narrative wherein consent is the key legal issue to be resolved; when it could not be resolved, the BCCA overturned O'Connor's conviction, thus precipitating the healing circle.

One of the main problems with laws concerning sexual assault is that they most often hinge on issues of consent, narrowly defined. Despite the emergence of a category of consent as part of feminist-inspired legal reforms that eliminated the need for victims to *physically* resist their perpetrators in order to prove rape, "a disjuncture between rules . . . and practice" nevertheless persists (Frohmann and Mertz 1994:833). As many feminist scholars have argued, the legal construction of rape as an issue of consent seriously limits how the victim can tell her story and how her story is interpreted, and it still often places the burden of proof on the victim to demonstrate how she *actively* did *not* consent to her assailant's sexual violence (Bridgeman and Millns 1998; Ehrlich 2001). As Susan Ehrlich argues in her analysis of American rape trials, "the overarching interpretive framework that . . . structured these proceedings was so seamless in its coverage that subaltern (i.e., victims') understandings of the events were rendered unrecognizable or imperceptible" (2001:1). Further, legal reforms involving sexual violence rarely, if ever, address how larger social structures and categories function in courtroom discourse, and how extant cultural scripts inform juridical procedure and interpretation.[24]

In this section, I supplement this gendered analysis of consent by arguing that the both Oppal's and the BCCA's decisions in *R. v. O'Connor* reveal consent to be not only an inadequate legal category, one which does not allow sufficient attention to be paid to the operation of factors such as race, gender, and colonization, but also a fundamentally ironic one because the relations that bring the indigenous complainants into prolonged contact with O'Connor were non-consensual. By constructing *R v. O'Connor* as a case about consent, legal discourse virtually erases colonial history, an erasure which rests on particular notions of temporality and subjectivity.

By denaturalizing the concept of consent, I want to shift the orientation of the question in O'Connor's case from "Did she consent or not?" to "What does consent look like when refracted through the prism of colonialism, in particular the residential school experience?" I demonstrate how the courts and the healing circle cannot be seen as discrete spheres; specifically, I argue that the courts' failure to properly resolve the issue of consent is what mobilizes the alternative, the healing circle, as a legitimate option. Further, the "bridging the cultural divide" discourse that epitomizes the healing circle is noticeably absent from the courts—an absence that is not peripheral to Oppal's and the BCCA's decisions, but rather constitutive of them.

In order to make these arguments, I first highlight some of these non-consensual acts and demonstrate how these not only shape and inform, but also bring about the conditions necessary for the sexual assaults to occur at all. Second, I discuss what I call the *temporality of consent*. I demonstrate how the courts locate the moment of violation in a very specific temporality, one occurring in a moment between two individuals, outside of any collective histories that shape such encounters (c.f. Razack 2002a; see also Deer 2004). Third, I ask how consent, and more specifically the consensual agent, is dependent on the erasure of indigeneity, sharply contrasting with the space of the healing circle which depends on the complainants' indigeneity in order to exist. I further explore the dichotomy between "erasing indigeneity" in one sphere and "becoming indigenous" in another.

CONSENT AND COLONIAL HISTORY

Consent in *R. v. O'Connor* is narrowly defined and limited to a particular set of legal issues. A key element in understanding *R v. O'Connor* is a broadening of the notion of consent to include historical and social forces that shape the relationships between O'Connor and the complainants. More specifically, the very conditions which both literally and historically brought O'Connor into long-term contact with the complainants epitomize *lack* of consent. I will briefly reference some well-traversed historical terrain in order to argue that issues of consent in this case must extend beyond where the law locates them: in a temporally-fixed interpersonal moment between two autonomous adult subjects. Rather, consent must be located in an understanding of BC's colonial history and postcolonial present, as well as in the context of what indigeneity had come to symbolize in late twentieth century multicultural Canada.

I first want to highlight some of the historical non-consensual acts that bring O'Connor into prolonged contact with the complainants and to demonstrate how they are part of the broader social conditions that shape and inform the contemporary context of O'Connor's case. In her discussion of the violent murder of Pamela George, an indigenous woman, at the hands of two white men, Razack reminds us that we must pay close attention to "the spatiality of the violence and its relationship to identity as well as to justice"(Razack 2002a:127). Her insight applies equally in O'Connor's case because a variety of factors including race, gender, and colonial history contribute to a specific spatial configuration necessary for the sexual assaults to occur at all.

While colonial encounters between indigenous groups and Europeans, and the results of such encounters, varied significantly depending on both chronological and regional factors, there were some general trends that shaped the overall experiences of colonization of indigenous peoples in Canada. For instance, colonial land policy resulted in the widespread and often illegal appropriation of indigenous territories by European colonial officials and settlers. This was non-consensual, especially in the context of BC.[25] The imposition of colonial British and later Canadian law was also non-consensual. As the RCAP report argues, this imposition resulted in far-reaching structural violence. It is this element of colonial history that the discourse of "bridging the cultural divide" is meant to address.

Perhaps most relevant to understanding *R. v. O'Connor* in historical perspective is that from 1879 until 1986, indigenous children were often removed from their families and communities without consent and placed in residential schools. Conditions in residential schools, sponsored by the government and run by Christian churches, were notoriously abusive, and many have argued that their long-term effects have devastated indigenous communities for generations. O'Connor was principal at the Cariboo Indian Residential School in Williams Lake, BC for many years, and all of the complainants were his students at some point in time.

CONSENT AND THE EFFECTS OF INDIAN RESIDENTIAL SCHOOLS IN CANADA

The Canadian government, in conjunction with Christian churches of different denominations, ran residential schools for indigenous children for over a century.[26] Part of the more general "civilizing mission" of imperial Indian policy, residential schools were created in the 1870s to assimilate indigenous children into the ways of settler society. Ideologically rooted in the colonial dichotomy of the savage Indian/civilized settler, education was seen as a critical step "to do away with the tribal system and assimilate the Indian people in all respects with the inhabitants of the Dominion, as speedily as they are fit to change."[27]

Most residential schools were located far away from indigenous communities so that the children could be "caught young to be saved from what is on the whole the degenerating influence of their home environment."[28] The government, encouraged by the churches, often forcibly removed children from their homes to live at the schools, and their parents were threatened with legal sanctions if they attempted to resist. While at school, the children were not permitted to speak their native languages, wear Indian clothes, or engage in other indigenous cultural practices. Further, Indian residential schools failed to provide the education they promised, and, throughout the history of the schools, the children were subject to systemic abuse and neglect.[29]

In recent years, former residential school students have made widespread allegations of rampant sexual abuse, especially on the part of clergy, and have filed a series of individual and class action lawsuits against the government participating churches. Additionally, an emergent group of personal narratives and academic writings has articulated the profound relationship between contemporary social and economic distress in indigenous communities and the residential school experience.[30]

To place O'Connor's healing circle in historical context, it is important to note that one of the stated purposes of the "civilizing mission" of residential schools was precisely to erase any "cultural" content from the lives of indigenous children. Residential schools were what sociologist Erving Goffman has famously termed "total institutions," institutions which use rigid structure, discipline, and isolation from wider communities to encompass the lives of inmates (1961).[31] Further, residential schools were premised on racialized beliefs about the inadequacy of indigenous cultures, and indeed of indigenous bodies; their entire existence was devoted to eradicating those cultures and changing (disciplining) those bodies. As historian John Milloy argues, "In thought and deed the establishment of this school system was an act of profound cruelty rooted in non-Aboriginal pride and intolerance and in the certitude and insularity of purported cultural superiority" (1999:302).

But what impact does this "civilizing mission" have on issues of consent in *R. v. O'Connor*? What relevance do residential schools and other colonial impositions have in understanding O'Connor's case, both from a legal perspective and otherwise? Foucault's concept of the *docile body* is illustrative here, especially in suggesting that the courts' treatment of O'Connor and the complainants as autonomous individuals without collective histories is deeply problematic. Foucault's genealogy of the docile body traces the discovery of "the body as object and target of power" and examines the "the body that is manipulated, shaped, trained, which obeys, responds, becomes skilful and increases its forces" (1995:136). The concept of docile bodies has great import in the discussion of the lingering effects of colonialism, especially in making the link between colonial structures and the individual lives of indigenous peoples. As Mary-Ellen Kelm argues in her discussion of the impact of colonization on health among BC's indigenous peoples, "The drama of colonization was acted out in Canada not only on the grand scale of treaty negotiations and reserve allocations but on the supple contours, the created representations, and the lived experiences of Aboriginal bodies" (1998:57). Her insight can be extended to the residential school system and its long-term impact on individual lives and bodies. The following analyses of the residential school system in Canada reveal how indigenous bodies became targets of power:

> The residential school system was, beyond question, intolerable. That inescapable reality was determined by the system's fundamental logic that called for the disruption of Aboriginal families and by the government's and churches' failure to parent the children in accordance with the standards of the day or to be vigilant guardians. As a result, all too often, "wards of the Department" were overworked, underfed, badly clothed, housed in unsanitary quarters, beaten with whips, rods and fists, chained and shackled, bound hand and foot, locked in closets, basements and bathrooms, and had their heads shaved or hair closely cropped (Milloy 1999:154–155).

Residential schools implemented a well-established technology that targeted the spirits, minds, feelings, and bodies of its wards. Its goal was not so much to create as to destroy; its product was designed, as far as possible, to be something not quite a person: something that would offer no intellectual or spiritual challenge to the oppressors, that might provide some limited service to its "masters" (should the "masters" desire it), and that would learn its place on the margins of Canadian society (Chrisjohn et al. 2002:76).

Such accounts of residential schools suggest the profound power over successive generations of indigenous children exercised by residential schools and their administrators. Clearly, the intersection between docile bodies and issues of consent is a multifaceted one, involving complex questions about the nature of agency, sexuality, and violence.[32] My aim here is not to resolve these questions, but rather suggest both the inadequacy and irony of the legal concept of consent in *R. v. O'Connor*. Consent is limited to a conception based on deracialized and selectively gendered identities as well as a profound lack of attention to colonial history and the larger structural forces which bring O'Connor and the complainants into a particular set of circumstances both at the time of the violations and, thirty years later, at the time of the law's intervention.

CONSENT IN *R. v. O'CONNOR* REVISITED

The legal issue at hand in *R. v. O'Connor* was whether or not the victims had consented to sexual relations with O'Connor, and if they had, whether or not that consent was vitiated by O'Connor's abuse of his authority. Except for the issue of O'Connor's authority in vitiating the complainants' consent, the courts treat the systematic oppression of residential schools as legally irrelevant. The specific nature of his authority is also not examined. His authority, however construed, is understood by the courts as something rooted in his individual positions as employer and priest rather than as part of a larger colonial structure. For instance, the legal narrative regarding the complainants' presence at the Cariboo Indian Residential School states the date they arrived and the age they were at that time. The circumstances under which the complainants "arrived" at the school remain unstated and unexamined.

Consent in this case is also articulated through cultural norms about sexuality. Sexual relations between white men and indigenous women have been naturalized throughout Canadian history; we thus must pay attention to how cultural norms are reflected in legal norms, and how these norms affect legal hermeneutics. In some important ways, the sexual acts between O'Connor and the complainants were naturalized, thus even further limiting the usefulness of consent. This context of normativity creates particular deracialized gendered subjectivities which take no account of colonial legacies and postcolonial realities. As many scholars have pointed out, the sexuality of indigenous women was at the heart of the colonial project in BC and elsewhere, and it was of particular concern to missionaries (see e.g., Barman 1997/98; Mawani 2002; Perry 2001; Razack 2002a; Stevenson 1995). In her discussion of O'Connor's case, historian Jean Barman argues:

> In British Columbia gender, power, and race came together in a manner that made it possible for men in power to condemn Aboriginal sexuality and at the same time, if they so chose, to use for their own gratification the very women they had turned into sexual objects (Barman 1997/98).

Razack further argues that an analysis of nineteenth century newspaper accounts demonstrates that there was a prevalent "conflation of Aboriginal woman and prostitute" as well as "an accompanying belief that when they encountered violence, Aboriginal women simply got what they deserved," a cultural script that continues to this day (2002a:131). One cannot ignore the denigrating cultural subtext of the hypersexualized indigenous woman when interpreting O'Connor's case.[33] For instance, a major legal hurdle for the complainants was that a significant amount of time had passed between the alleged violations and the court cases. Some of the complainants articulated their deep fear and ambivalence about coming forward at the time of the violations. While Oppal argued that despite certain inconsistencies about places and dates in the complainants' testimony, their narratives nevertheless had "the ring of truth," the BCCA found these inconsistencies especially troublesome.

Arguably, O'Connor's violations were further normalized by a tacit, although pervasive, assumption, namely, that chastity is an 'unnatural' state for a man. In such a view, a priest engaging in sexual relations with young, adult *women*, while not preferable, would nevertheless be understandable. In his trial, O'Connor either denied that the alleged events took place at all or asserted that he had been seduced by the complainants. His assertion that he was seduced by his students and employees intersected with the script of the hypersexualized indigenous woman.

THE TEMPORALITY OF CONSENT

We must also pay attention to the specific temporality on which all of the legal concepts of consent referenced by the court rest. Such legal constructions also largely ignore the spatial dimensions of colonialism and gender oppression. More specifically, the court does not reference the historical circumstances which bring O'Connor into contact with the complainants nor does it recognize the epistemological conditions which create the legal hermeneutics of which consent is a part. For instance, liberal ideology provides a context for the courts to interpret Belleau and O'Connor's sexual relationship as "a contract between autonomous individuals standing outside of history" (Razack 2002a:156).

Both Oppal and the BCCA discuss a variety of legal precedents involving issues of consent in order to determine whether or not the complainants gave their consent. Both courts also rely on specific temporalities to narrate and understand the events in question, and thus create a particular legal subjectivity that is disconnected from larger structures and discourses. They each construct a certain sequence of events as interpersonal moments between two individuals. Harm or violation occurs in that moment, and it is only that moment that gets named legally. The issue of consent is then abstracted from these events.

This kind of temporality locates *a* moment of violation, enabling the separation of an individual moment from a larger social field. Such a construction presumes not only a normative legal subjectivity, but also a particular relationship between subjects constructed at a specific moment in time. In both the rape and indecent assault claims, each offence is related to the *first* sexual encounter between O'Connor and the complainants, as though issues of consent did not apply to subsequent ones.

According to trial testimony, the sexual relationship between O'Connor and Belleau lasted for some time, and resulted in the birth of a daughter, given up for adoption. When placed in this context, it is not easy to locate a precise moment of violation or of consent. Such an analysis should not suggest a radical lack of agency on the part of the complainants; rather, the legal construction of consent (and consent as the key legal issue) is deeply problematic because it relies on a particular mobilization of legal subjectivity which presumes not only a rational subject, but also one largely free of embodied constraints and pressures. As Larissa Behrendt argues in her discussion of Aboriginal women in Australia, "the ability to exercise consent and agency within the colonial context should not obscure the constraints imposed by colonial structures (and their legacies) on the lives of Aboriginal women" (Behrendt 2000:365).

Again, Oppal attempts to account for some of these in his discussion of how O'Connor's authority as priest, principal, and employer vitiates the consent of the complainants. Nevertheless, both Oppal's and the BCCA's omission of any general discussion of colonial history and of any specific discussion of the residential school experience seriously limits their understanding because some of the most relevant evidence was not included in their evaluation. More specifically, there was no probing into larger issues that inform the events in question. For instance, which structural and discursive relations bring O'Connor into contact with the complainants? How does the residential school experience shape O'Connor's and the complainants' understandings of self and their interactions with one another? Why would women who ostensibly consented to sex thirty years before bring a case so many years later?

Regardless of the differences between Oppal's and the BCCA's decisions, both of them locate consent in an interpersonal moment between individual actors, and both make a determination through a limited view of events, abstracted precedents, and evaluations of O'Connor's and the complainants' testimony. In this sense, *R. v. O'Connor* proceeded in typical legal fashion. Yet some larger questions remain. For example, why, and through what processes, were inquiries about the nature of residential schools excluded? What would consent look like if refracted through these kinds of questions? Could the legal discourse evoked by the courts hold in this context? The *temporality of consent* used in both the provincial court and the Court of Appeal seriously limits the kinds of questions asked, and this temporality rests on the erasure of indigeneity.

THE ERASURE OF INDIGENEITY IN CANADIAN COURTS

In order to explain how "consent could be vitiated by the exercise of authority," Oppal contextualizes the moment of violation, arguing that factors such as age, religion, and economic need mitigated Belleau's consent. Yet even this contextualization of consent, one sympathetic to Belleau, is problematic:

> . . . her apparent failure to resist his advances is entirely understandable when one considers their relative backgrounds and positions. The complainant went to a residential school when she was 6 years old. As a Catholic, she was taught to respect and obey the priests who were authority figures. Father O'Connor was not only her priest but was also her employer. Father O'Connor was highly respected by the students and former students. As Ms. [S.] said, "We knew our place." In the circumstances it would have been extremely difficult for her to resist his demands (1998:par. 25).

The judge's account of the complainant's "apparent failure to resist his advances" is deracialized and removed from any explicit discussion of the conditions of residential schools and attendant colonial ideologies. Thus, even in an attempt to legitimate the complainant's account of events, Oppal constructs an account that conceptualizes the problem in terms of less risky categories: Belleau's age and O'Connor's position as principal, employer, and priest. In fact, the only explicit reference to race in *R. v. O'Connor* came from testimony originally given by Marilyn Belleau in the 1996 trial wherein she describes O'Connor's "really white body" (1998:par. 20). Thus, Oppal's decision is not only *not* framed in terms of colonial oppression, but also completely deracialized as though these issues were separate from the question as to whether or not she legally consented. The erasure of indigeneity in *R v. O'Connor* enables the erasure of entire histories of colonization. In stark contrast to the healing circle, which depends on indigeneity to function as an "alternative" space, the courts construct an account that is virtually without reference to the complainants' indigeneity.

CONCLUSION

Both Oppal, through appeal to Anglo common law tradition, and the judges on the Court of Appeal, through appeal to the absence of explicit statutes, wrote legally compelling decisions in O'Connor's case yet came to very different determinations. To answer one of the questions that oriented this chapter—namely, "What does consent look like when refracted through the prism of colonialism, in particular the residential school experience?"—we must look to the similarities rather than the differences between the decisions. Neither involved any explicit discussion of colonial history. To convict O'Connor, Justice Oppal accepted the Crown's contention that any submission to O'Connor's advances on the part of the complainants was vitiated by the exercise of authority. The defense team countered that in O'Connor's case the exercise of authority could not vitiate consent because the concept was not in the Criminal Code at the time of the alleged offenses. Colonial relations were not a factor in the BCCA's decision to overturn O'Connor's conviction nor were they an explicit factor in Oppal's original decision to convict him.

O'Connor's healing circle, when viewed as part of an emerging pattern within a multicultural imaginary reflected in law, is not so anomalous. It functions to deny precisely what it is supposed to be addressing: the ongoing effects of colonization on indigenous communities as they struggle for greater self-determination. By formulating these issues in terms of an ahistoricized cultural difference, the discourse of "bridging the cultural divide" as it manifests in O'Connor's healing circle reinforces extant colonial relations. One of the main arguments made by proponents of culturally-specific indigenous restorative justice initiatives is that the forcible imposition of colonial, and later Canadian law, was also non-consensual. Thus, indigenous restorative justice is, at least in part, meant to address the often violent imposition of colonial law on indigenous communities by revitalizing traditional forms in contemporary contexts. Yet, as the specific contours of O'Connor's healing circle demonstrate, attempts to address the profound impact of colonial laws and policies on indigenous communities have been hindered by multicultural imaginings that interpret these relations through a culturalized discourse that downplays or effaces the very relations it is supposed to be addressing.

The over-determined construction of the healing circle as a space wherein the legal subject "becomes indigenous" can only exist in opposition to a mainstream court system in which indigeneity is seen as irrelevant to its operation. More specifically, the structural position of indigenous women is irrelevant to the way in which the legal category of consent is constructed and deployed in mainstream courts. The process of "erasing indigeneity" in these legal contexts is in fact an erasure of entire histories of colonization and their consequences. It is precisely the erasure of indigeneity in the mainstream courts that allows the healing circle, a place wherein indigeneity is ostensibly celebrated, to take place at all. Thus, "indigenous becoming" in one legal sphere rests on its erasure in another. The healing circle was the only forum wherein discussions of residential school experience were allowed, wherein connections between O'Connor's violations of the complainants and the broader violations of residential schools were articulated. Yet, despite any benefit that the complainants may have received, the healing circle was legally irrelevant. In other words, it did nothing to reconfigure the relationships and subjectivities produced in the courts. Instead, it reproduced these relationships and subjectivities in ways that simultaneously fit a statist multicultural imaginary and downplayed or denied the structural violence of postcolonial realities.[34]

4   Resettling Musqueam Park
Property, Culture, and Difference in *Glass v. Musqueam Indian Band*

Reserve land worth half of market value
The Supreme Court of Canada assessed 40 acres of prime Vancouver real estate at half its market value yesterday solely because the leased land was located on an Indian reserve. A 5–4 majority said each lease-holder in the leafy residential neighbourhood near the University of British Columbia campus must pay the Musqueam Indian band about $10,000 annually—half the amount they would have paid without the political uncertainty and potential unrest of an Indian reserve. "This fact cannot be dismissed or ignored," Mr. Justice Charles Gon-thier wrote. "In the future, the market may respond differently. But when the market perceives uncertainty, it is cold comfort to the lessor to believe that the lessees' fears are unwarranted." Kerry-Lynne Find-lay, a Musqueam leaseholder and spokesperson for the group of 73 elated leaseholders, said the decision is "a victory" for non-aboriginal people that will reverberate across the country. She estimated about 60,000 non-aboriginal people, mostly in Ontario, hold leases on land in Indian reserves [*The Globe and Mail*, November 2000].[1]

INTRODUCTION

Musqueam Park is an affluent residential subdivision nestled on forty acres of the Musqueam Indian Reserve 2 (IR2) in the city of Vancouver, British Columbia (BC). Comprised of comfortable single-family homes on leafy, oversized lots, Musqueam Park was for decades prized by residents for its central location and proximity to some of the city's most beautiful green spaces. Yet in 1995, an intense struggle over land rents emerged between the Musqueam Indian Band and its non-indigenous tenants. Over the next five years, the resulting battle—in the courts, in the media, and in the pub-lic sphere—significantly reshaped the value, legal standing, and cultural meaning of Musqueam Park. In late 2000, the Supreme Court of Canada (SCC) handed down a split decision in *Musqueam Indian Band v. Glass* ([2000] 2 S.C.R.; hereafter *Glass*). In *Glass*, the court maintained that because of its *sui generis* character, "Indian land" was significantly less

valuable than other privately-held forms of property and discounted leasehold rents owed to the Band by 50 percent.

In a recent volume, anthropologists Katherine Verdery and Caroline
Humphrey (2004) advocate close attention to how various concepts of
property operate in specific settings and to "what sort of work a property
concept is doing when it seems to acquire new amplitude" (Humphrey and
Verdery 2004:3). Following their lead, I look at how Musqueam Park is
constituted as "Indian land" in the context of this dispute. How is its value
legally constructed and publicly legitimated? How do characteristics originally ascribed to reserve land in the nineteenth century—inalienability,
collective ownership, Aboriginal title—acquire a novel salience at the end
of the twentieth? More specifically, by using the concept of *landscape*—
as both a "physical space" and "a way of seeing" (Blomley 1998:568)—I
explore how the value of Musqueam Park is constituted through a variety
of discursive and material practices that reinscribe colonial property relations and help maintain settler access to Indian lands. In this chapter, I
examine Musqueam Park's historical emergence as a desirable residential
area for almost exclusively non-indigenous homeowners and its shifting
boundaries and inscriptions in light of the Musqueam attempt to collect
higher rents. I argue that embedded in this political and legal dispute are a
series of factors that further landscape Musqueam Park. These include the
following:(1) how settler anxieties about shifting power dynamics between
indigenous and settler societies, including concerns about changing structures of governance, access to land, and resource allocation, shape the discursive content of the dispute; (2) how the historical underdevelopment of
reserves in general, and the Musqueam reserve in particular, sets the stage
for contemporary battles over valuable residential property; and, (3) how
colonial relations, especially in terms of property, continue to shape public
and legal discourses in BC.

PROPERTY AND DIFFERENCE

In 1995, the Musqueam Indian Band, a First Nation with just over a thousand registered members and three urban reserves around Vancouver,
sued a group of its tenants in federal court in an attempt to collect outstanding land rents. The tenants, more commonly known as *leaseholders*,
were a group of seventy-three affluent non-Indian homeowners living in
Musqueam Park.

While the leaseholders owned their homes and held ninety-nine-year
leaseholds to Musqueam Park property, the Band maintained collective title
to the underlying land. Originally negotiated in 1965 by the federal government on the Band's behalf, the leases were part of a burgeoning movement
to promote economic development on reserves and generate income for
Band members. For the first thirty years of the leases, the leaseholders paid

small fixed annual rents (approximately CAN$300-$400 per year). The leases specified, however, that in 1995 the method for calculating annual rents was to change. Rather than fixed rents, the Band and the leaseholders were directed to negotiate a "fair rent" based on six percent of the "current land value" of the property (*Glass*, 1).

Because of the (originally) advantageous lease terms, desirable location, and booming Vancouver housing market, land rents in Musqueam Park were set to increase by more than five thousand percent in 1995, jumping from $400 to approximately $36,000 per year. Panicked leaseholders argued that these increases would displace them from their homes and lead them to financial ruin. The Band countered that despite leaseholder claims to the contrary, the increases were legitimate, not only reflective of property values in the area, but also supported by common law real estate practice.

The proposed jump in rents was a substantial one, and leaseholders expressed understandable concerns about their financial well-being. Yet, what is of particular interest in this case is *how* the leaseholders asserted their claim to Musqueam Park and to discounted rents. The legal crux of the dispute rested on how properly to appraise the value of the land in order to calculate the new rents. The leaseholders argued that because of its status as "Indian land," as land that was collectively owned, inalienable, and subject to Aboriginal title, Musqueam Park was not analogous to neighboring fee simple land, and consequently should not be appraised as such. The Band countered that common law practice supported its contention that "current land value" should reflect the price that the land would get if it were to be sold on the open market. In *Glass*, the Supreme Court upheld an earlier federal decision that argued that because of its location on reserve land, Musqueam Park properties should be appraised at fifty percent of the value of similarly situated fee simple land. Following the arguments of the original trial judge and the leaseholders, the SCC's majority found that leasehold reserve land constituted not only a *sui generis* category of property, but also a less valuable one.

Between 1995 and 2000, the struggle over rents in Musqueam Park reverberated across Canada. Emerging at a time when many First Nations were battling for legal recognition of their rights to land, resources, and self-determination, issues involving indigenous peoples were perceived to be particularly threatening by many non-indigenous Canadians, especially in the province of BC. Leaseholders argued that they were victims not only of unscrupulous profiteering on the part of the Band, but also of reckless government policies willing to sacrifice the rights of "ordinary" citizens in a wrong-headed and discriminatory attempt to bring closure to the longstanding claims of indigenous peoples (Frank 2000). Debates about "fair rent" and "current land value" exceeded the boundaries of the courtroom, often becoming deeply racialized debates about *what* and *who* were fair and valuable.

Not only was the clash over Musqueam Park a high-profile dispute, revealing some of the cleavages extant in Canadian settler society, but it was also an important decision in Canadian law, marking a significant moment in indigenous legal history. During the past thirty years, many indigenous claims, both in legal and extra-legal spheres, have been articulated using an idiom of *difference*. The idiom of difference refers to self-conscious, explicitly cultural claims that emphasize the idea of epistemological distance between indigenous and settler cultures. Within this context, the notion of cultural difference has been particularly useful in pointing out assumptions embedded in ostensibly neutral institutions such as law and in revealing the power inequities inhering in them. Yet the idiom of difference takes on a novel role in *Glass*: an appeal to the legal relevance of indigenous difference was mobilized not by the Musqueam themselves, but rather by the leaseholders. Although not originally an indigenous rights case, legal discourse in *Glass* transformed it into one, creating a precedent that could have potentially profound effects for how reserve land is understood and valued in the future. In light of burgeoning non-indigenous populations on reserves and reservations across North America, I suggest that the court's conception of the status of Indian land has the effect of a twenty-first century *resettlement*. While certainly not a straightforward reiteration of earlier colonial forms in the province, the resettlement of Musqueam Park bears some striking similarities to the circumstances surrounding colonization in BC in the late nineteenth and early twentieth centuries. These include clashes between settler and indigenous populations about legitimate access to land and its appropriate uses, the central role of law and legal idioms in the articulation of rights and property, and the contested role that indigenous peoples occupy (and are allowed to occupy) in capitalist enterprises.

In *Glass*, the Band articulated its claim in commensurable terms, in the capitalist idiom of Canadian property law, seeking legally to maximize its profit in Musqueam Park. In contrast to other First Nations' claims in recent high-profile Supreme Court cases, the Musqueam did not go before the Court to seek legal recognition of their *difference*, but rather asked it to recognize their *sameness* before the law. Yet the leaseholders contended, and the Supreme Court ultimately agreed, that indigenous difference was a key part of "Indian land," and thus fundamental to the legal resolution in Musqueam Park.

THE LANDSCAPE OF MUSQUEAM PARK

In his article, "Landscapes of Property," cultural geographer Nicholas Blomley probes the relationship between space and power, asking how space, specifically property, is socially constituted especially in the context of struggle (1998). Asserting the importance of both the material and the representational in understanding property relations, he uses the metaphor of *landscape* to discuss ongoing clashes over gentrification in Vancouver's marginalized Downtown Eastside.[2] Blomley reminds us that *landscapes* "allow us to think through the material production of space, while recognizing the manner in which that space is visualized and represented" (1998:585). I extend these insights here to another Vancouver site in order to trace the spatial and historical emergence of Musqueam Park as a way to contextualize the SCC's decision asserting that "Indian land" is less valuable than comparable property.

PROPERTY VALUES IN MUSQUEAM PARK

Not only were leaseholders protected from sharp increases in land rents during the first thirty years of the leases, but they also benefited from rising real estate values. In 1990, homes in Musqueam Park regularly sold for between $450,000 and $600,000, values that matched pace with the west side's boom, and were comparable to nearby freehold properties (Armstrong 2000). Despite the impending changes to leasehold rent calculations, properties in Musqueam Park continued to sell strongly well into the early nineties, a factor likely attributable to a commonly held perception among leaseholders and potential buyers that rents would not increase substantially after 1995. In his study of leaseholder purchasing behavior between 1980 and 1998, Derek Armstrong contends: "Leaseholders in Musqueam Park treated their leaseholdings as if they were equity in the same sense that a freehold property would be. Leaseholders expected to be able to sell 'their' property and homes for amounts comparable to the market prices for freehold properties" (2000:2–3). Thus, during the first thirty years of the leases, Musqueam Park properties held something akin to freehold value, which, generated by the homes *and the land,* adhered almost exclusively to the leaseholders.

Prior to 1995, there was very little public concern expressed about the impending rent increase, despite the fact that it was common knowledge in the area (Constantineau 1990; Bruce Miller 2000:personal communication). In 1995, the mainstream media *en masse* began to report on the dispute in Musqueam Park. Many of the news stories and editorials focused on the uncertainty surrounding the dispute and its negative impact on property values.

Throughout 1999, public discussion of the dispute heightened. Mainstream media described the "drastic" and "sudden" nature of the rent increases, often downplaying or forgetting the very specific terms of the lease; they also rarely reported that the Band was negotiating a fixed lease rate for the next twenty years, again without any compensation for inflation or potential growth in land values. Instead, a series of alarmist editorials presented the Musqueam Band as conspiratorial, opportunistic, and avaricious.[3]

Missing from this description of Musqueam Park, however, is an account of how such a desirable and valuable residential space materialized on reserve land. In the following sections, I give a brief account of the emergence of Musqueam Park and discuss some of the racialized discourses surrounding the dispute in the context of the Supreme Court's decision in *Glass*. I ask not only how the historical and spatial configuration of Musqueam Park links with legal encodings of property and value, but also how the historical underdevelopment of reserves in general, and the Musqueam reserve in particular, sets the stage for contemporary battles over valuable residential property.

"PROPERTY OF THE WHITE PEOPLE FOREVER": RESERVES IN BRITISH COLUMBIA

> The national mythologies of white settler societies are deeply spatialized stories. Although the spatial story that is told varies from one time to another, at each stage the story installs Europeans as entitled to the land, a claim codified in law [Razack 2002b:3].

Legal scholar Cheryl Harris has famously argued that "whiteness and property share a common premise—a conceptual nucleus—of a right to exclude" (1993:1714). Through an examination of the emergence of whiteness and the evolution of American property law in relation to the exclusion of Blacks and Native Americans from these spheres, Harris asserts that race and property are inextricably linked, contending that a privileged concept of whiteness comes to be "embedded . . . into the very definition of property" (1993:1721; see also Wolfe 2001). Thus "American law has a recognized property interest in whiteness," one which creates unacknowledged conditions "against which legal disputes are framed, argued, and adjudicated" (Harris 1993:1714). I extend Harris's insights to encompass Canadian law, arguing that "a property interest in whiteness" frames the Musqueam Park dispute, creating a nexus of symbolic and material conditions through which both the controversy and the Supreme Court's decision are articulated.

Race profoundly structures Canadian law and society, yet there are discursive conditions which severely limit discussion of these issues (see e.g., Aylward 1999; Backhouse 1999). For instance, it is a longstanding myth, oft-reproduced in history textbooks, news media, and other sources, that Canada has been gentler with the indigenous peoples now encompassed by its boundaries than have other nation-states, most notably the US. While this myth has been debunked, or at the very least problematized, in academic and activist literatures, it is nevertheless prevalent in public discourse and still frames the reception of many First Nations' claims.

In Canada, as in other postcolonial nations, the racial categories of white and Indian have been mutually constitutive; that is, these categories developed in tandem with each other. This has been the case historically and it is still the case now. There is a burgeoning literature in Canadian critical race theory that deals specifically with the racial construction of indigenous peoples, specifically the prevalent native/non-native dichotomy that is more familiar in Canadian race relations. As Carol Schick argues, "[T]he construction of white-identified people is established through the production of Aboriginal peoples as Other" (2002:105–106). Unlike the US, however, it is relatively rare in public discourse in Canada to speak overtly about race in reference to either indigenous peoples or whites; rather, "culture" is the preferred term used to evoke specific kinds of difference, often effacing the racialized (and gendered) dimensions of Canadian society, and thus limiting critical intervention in larger questions about racism and equality. Building on the work of earlier critical race theorists, Sherene Razack calls this process "culturalization," arguing that in these circumstances "[c]ulture then becomes the framework used by white society to pre-empt both racism and sexism" (1998:60).

Concepts of race have a long history in British Columbia, and while these concepts have been by no means monolithic or necessarily coherent, they have been nevertheless consistently premised on settler assertions of difference from, and superiority to, indigenous peoples. At the time of early resettlement during the mid-nineteenth century, British colonial officials envisioned their westernmost colonies in racial terms by imagining them as white spaces, the creation of which would require the formation of sharp legal and spatial divisions between indigenous and white populations.

An oft-cited fact about BC's racial history is that a series of treaties negotiated with indigenous peoples on Vancouver Island in the 1850s stated that the purchased land would become "property of the White people for ever" (Tennant 1990:xi). This assertion locates, in early colonial law, the desire for difference among white settler populations in BC, a desire intimately linked with notions of race and of property, and one which has been present throughout BC's history. Paul Tennant points out that from the early days of resettlement until the postwar era, "Whites in the province were eager to distinguish themselves from non-Whites," in part as a way of protecting their political and material interests (1990:xi). These distinctions were organized and expressed in a variety of ways, and they were especially manifest in the racial, spatial, and legal dimensions of property.[4]

Historical geographer Cole Harris makes the argument that nineteenth century white resettlement in BC coincides with some important shifts in the trajectory of British colonial thought, shifts which reformulated concepts of race and humanity, thus differently shaping the form and experience of colonization in western Canada. He points to the diminishing popularity of the liberal humanitarian tradition in the 1840s and 50s, a tradition which, although premised on the inferiority of indigenous peoples, still presumed a "universalistic vision of a common humanity" (2002:10). However, an increasing reliance on evolving "scientific" arguments about racial difference (specifically the racial immutability and inferiority of non-Europeans) slowly emerged and eroded this perception of a common humanity (Harris 2002:11). As these new racial concepts gained currency, colonial attitudes about indigenous peoples grew more negative. Further, throughout the colonized world, a growth in white immigrant populations was concurrent with a decline in indigenous ones, the latter having been subjected to the ravaging effects of often violent colonial policies and European diseases. This historical moment buttressed white settler beliefs both in the biological inferiority of indigenous peoples and in the idea that these peoples represented a dying race. Thus there was a pervasive colonial belief in the inferiority (and fundamental difference) of indigenous peoples, a belief that undergirded colonial law and policy especially in the realm of property.

Property was a central organizing metaphor for colonial ideology. Historically, private property was considered to be exclusive to Europeans, and it was widely believed that indigenous peoples either had a very primitive understanding of property, or had none at all. Colonizers justified the appropriation of indigenous territories by asserting that these lands were either uninhabited (*terra nullius*) or underused (Culhane 1998). As both Peter Fitzpatrick (2000) and Patricia Seed (2001) point out, even when confronted with contradictory evidence (i.e. indigenous agrarians), colonists either ignored this evidence or they reconstructed concepts and laws which continued to relegate indigenous peoples to lower forms, outside of political society and property. As historian Seed suggests:

> Those taking others' property needed to see a clearly defined boundary between themselves and the others to justify seizing assets belonging to those others. If the line dividing the two were indistinguishable, then the colonizer's certainty about their right to seize resources might vanish, or at least become open to question (2001:116).

Thus concepts of private property themselves evolved in relation to these kinds of colonial encounters and the presumed inferiority of indigenous peoples. Echoes of these colonial encounters reverberate in the dispute over Musqueam Park. For instance, settler discourse has often relied on "higher use" arguments to justify appropriation of indigenous territories. Higher use claims have persisted in contemporary settler-indigenous conflicts over land and resources (Miller 1998). In the case of Musqueam Park, such claims are confounded by the Band's attempts to put the land to its "highest use" by seeking maximum profit.

In her discussion of mixed-race identity in colonial British Columbia, sociologist Renisa Mawani (2002) suggests that late nineteenth century Canadian legal definitions of "Indian" were not simply a reflection of racial categories extant in settler society, but rather were also ways of protecting government interests in Indian land. She examines those late nineteenth and early twentieth century legal definitions of "Indian-ness" that relied on blood quantum, arguing that by restricting the ability of mixed-race people to assert indigenous claims to land, these definitions "linked blood with *real* property and citizenship" (2002:56). Mawani argues that because it increased the number of people who could claim Native ancestry, and thus the number of people who would have a right to reserve land under the preceding legal regime, the social phenomenon of "race-mixing in British Columbia potentially jeopardized European efforts to appropriate indigenous land" (2002:50). As a result, the federal government became progressively more restrictive in its legal definitions of who was and was not "Indian," thus limiting the amount of land it was legally required to allocate for reserves. An important insight in Mawani's work, then, is that colonial anxiety about mixed-race progeny cannot be construed as merely symbolic or metaphorical concerns about racial purity; rather, this anxiety was also deeply rooted in material concerns about land (see also Perry 2001). The racialized fear and anxiety expressed by the leaseholders and other settler Canadians during the Musqueam dispute are also deeply rooted in material concerns about land, concerns ultimately mitigated by the Supreme Court's decision in *Glass*.

Although the Musqueam reserve itself was not created until 1870, the legal and political foundations of Musqueam Park were laid early, as early as the Royal Proclamation of 1763. In the Proclamation, the British Crown codified the concept of *Indian title* (now called *Aboriginal title*), distinguishing it from other types of property recognized in common law. Indian title differed in three important ways from the typical British fee simple title granted to white settlers, and these differences "sharply curtailed the freedom of the Indians to do as they wished with their lands" (Tennant 1990:11). First, Indian title would be held collectively as opposed to individually. Second, unlike fee simple land, Indian land could not be bought or sold on an open market; rather, it could only be transferred to the Crown for sale or negotiation. Finally, Indian title was *recognized* rather than created by the Crown, and was thus considered to be a codification of "aboriginal arrangements" predating European colonization (ibid.).

Described as "the province's most basic colonial spaces," BC's reserves were established between 1850 and 1938, and currently comprise half of one percent of the province's land base (Harris 2002:xxi). Because the reserve system emerged over a long period of time, under the direction of different colonial regimes, its development was not monolithic; yet for nearly a century, the establishment of Indian reserves was a key element of the colonizing project in BC. The relegation of indigenous peoples to a mere fraction of their traditional territories enabled European settlers to appropriate the majority of land in the province for their own use and to exert greater control over resistant indigenous populations. Reserves were not, however, simply manifestations of self-interested economic or political policy; they were also legally circumscribed spaces of segregation, premised on the inferiority and radical difference of indigenous peoples (Tennant 1990:11).

As we will see below, it is this premise of inferiority and radical difference that is ultimately reinscribed by the SCC's decision in *Glass*. Despite the Band's commensurable claims in the form of common law real estate practices and the desire for profit, the SCC imposed incommensurability on Musqueam Park—expressed in the legal category of *leasehold reserve land*—an incommensurability that ultimately provides justification for the court's decision to discount rents.

THE EMERGENCE OF MUSQUEAM PARK

When the Musqueam Reserve lands were surveyed and allotted in the 1870s, no one could have known how valuable the land on IR 2 would become.[5] However, by 1956, the federal government noted that the reserve lands were ripe for development and that they were "the most potentially valuable 400 acres in Vancouver today" (*Guerin v. The Queen*, [1984] 2 S.C.R. 335).

From their inception until well into the twentieth century, most reserve lands throughout Canada were isolated from economic development. Often remote, resource-poor, and lacking in capital, reserves were seen as economic hinterlands. Many First Nations peoples were required to leave them in order to seek educational and employment opportunities elsewhere. During the 1950s and 1960s, however, the federal government created a series of development schemes to promote economic growth on reserves and to provide alternative sources of income for First Nations.

When Musqueam Park was created during the 1960s, developers were predicting big things for the area. A private development company called the remaining land within IR 2 "the most valuable undeveloped acreage remaining within the City limits of Vancouver" (Rawson & Wiles 1967:23). Musqueam Park's potential value as a residential subdivision inhered in its simultaneous proximity to "pristine natural" rainforests and beaches and "urban" cityscapes such as the University of British Columbia, affluent residential neighborhoods on the west side, and downtown Vancouver.

The Band was among the first in the nation to lease land to settler Canadians for residential purposes. Yet, under the terms of the federal government's *Indian Act*, Bands could not negotiate business deals on their own behalf; rather, they needed to legally "surrender" their interests in reserve land to the federal government, who then in turn could sell or develop the reserve on behalf of the Band. The Musqueam Band conditionally surrendered its interest in the land that would eventually become Musqueam Park to the federal government in 1960. The government was responsible for negotiating with a private company to develop the land into a residential subdivision, the proceeds of which would go to the Band. While the Musqueam Band Council was involved with the development of the subdivision, it was ultimately the federal government's responsibility to arrange for lease terms that it felt were most conducive to the welfare of the Band. The level of involvement of the Band Council in the original negotiations and the federal government's desire or ability to arrange for a good financial deal for the Musqueam back in 1965 are still matters of dispute. It is nevertheless clear that land values in southwest Vancouver increased substantially during the ensuing thirty years, but that this boom did not result in commensurable profits for the Band.

Ironically, the Musqueam reserve's chronic economic underdevelopment, which had preserved its "natural" feel for nearly a century, enabled the creation of a residential space of great desirability and value. In the 1980s, another form of landscaping further added to the value of Musqueam Park: the creation of Pacific Spirit Regional Park.

PACIFIC SPIRIT REGIONAL PARK

> From estuary marshes, rock and cobble beaches, wooded ravines, upland forests and ancient bog—take your pick! Hike along rugged shores next to the ocean. Wander barefoot on shining tidal flats or sunbathe among scattered driftwood to the sound of lapping waves. Spot eagles perched majestically in gnarled, gray snags; their sharp eyes scanning the Fraser River, Howe Sound and English Bay. Climb steep trails past narrow ravines onto the forested plateau where most trails are suitable for hikers, cyclists and horseback riders. Tall cedar, hemlock and Douglas-fir are mixed with bright patches of bitter cherry, red alder and maple. The seasons highlight lush evergreens, brilliant colours or frosty branches.
>
> Description of Pacific Spirit Regional Park
> [Dunbar Residents' Association, n.d.]

A key part of the Musqueam Park landscape is its contiguity with Vancouver's third largest green space: the stunning Pacific Spirit Regional Park. Like other parts of the city, Pacific Spirit Park emerged in a context of contestation wherein a series of groups made opposing claims to urban space in attempts to reclaim, preserve, gentrify, and develop.[6]

In 1907, the province created the University Endowment Lands (UEL) by appropriating approximately three thousand densely forested acres on the Point Grey peninsula. The UEL were then used to establish British Columbia's first university, now the University of British Columbia (UBC). Despite longstanding Musqueam claims that this land composed part of their traditional territory, the province refused either to enter into an agreement with or to offer compensation to the Musqueam Band (Musqueam Indian Band 1989).

In the ensuing decades, UBC expanded and thrived, and the surrounding locales became some of the most prestigious and valuable residential

areas in the city. In response to a proposal for more housing on undeveloped UEL tracts in 1987, local residents and environmentalists suc-
cessfully lobbied the provincial government to transfer land title to the
Greater Vancouver Regional District (GVRD) in order to create a protected green space. The Musqueam Band, concerned that such a transfer
jeopardized its still unsettled land claims, tried unsuccessfully in 1987 to
prevent the transfer. The Band argued that it had "never sold or been compensated for its interests in the land and resources" nor had it "stopped
using the UEL land and resources for sustenance and for cultural and religious purposes" (Musqueam Indian Band 1989:1). In 1989, a BC appeals
court refused to grant an injunction preventing the transfer. Although
the GVRD requested that the transfer transpire without prejudice to any
Musqueam claims, the province refused, and Pacific Spirit Regional Park
was created in April of that year.

The creation of Pacific Spirit Regional Park is central to understanding
the contemporary landscape of Musqueam Park because it is undeniable,
at least in this context, that the subdivision's proximity to a large green
space positively impacts property values. The ability for urban dwellers
to quickly escape "to estuary marshes, rock and cobble beaches, wooded
ravines, upland forests and ancient bog" is highly prized. Additionally, the
containment of further housing development in the area helps make properties like those in Musqueam Park increasingly rare. Thus, part of the
value of Musqueam Park properties is that they are surrounded by a "natural" environment, by a "pristine" landscape claimed unsuccessfully by the
Band and indefinitely protected under current legal regimes.

"ETHNIC CLEANSING BY FISCAL MEANS":
LEASEHOLDER CLAIMS TO MUSQUEAM PARK

While the Band employed a kind of color-blind discourse to argue its position, asserting that the dispute was nothing more than a "private contract
matter" (Kesselman 1999), the leaseholders appealed to the government and
the courts to protect them from what they characterized as "apartheid" and
"ethnic cleansing by fiscal means."[7] Through the evocation of terms such as
"ethnic cleansing" and "apartheid," leaseholders presented themselves as
the victims of *race*-based oppression, a discursive move that simultaneously
effaces their economic and political privilege *and* casts aspersions on the
moral legitimacy of the Band's legal claims. To focus on power inequities
inherent in the landlord-tenant relationship would be unsettling to both the
symbolic and material capital of the leaseholders. Leaseholder discourse,
then, focuses not on the possibility of displacement itself, but rather who is
potentially displaced by whom in Musqueam Park.

Settler societies have relied, both materially and symbolically, on the
displacement of indigenous peoples for the settlement of "new" colonial

territories. When confronted with political and legal challenges from indigenous groups, settler societies have developed narratives to make sense of them (Dominy 1995; Furniss 1997/98; Furniss 1999). In Canada, the idiom of cultural difference has enabled settler mentality to maintain clear distinctions between indigenous and non-indigenous, between Indians and other Canadians, often to the exclusion of any nuanced understanding of the complex political and cultural dynamics that inform situations like the Musqueam Park dispute (Furniss 1999:15). In this section, I provide a brief mapping of the terrain of cultural difference in Canada, and examine how it is expressed through claims to property. More specifically, I analyze how the leaseholders and other settler Canadians narrated the dispute in deeply racialized ways, and suggest that they deployed concepts of difference to create a moral discourse legitimizing settler claims to Indian land.

Distinctions like "native/non-native" and "native/ordinary Canadian" are common in Canadian public discourse. Such concepts are necessary to the settler Canadian imaginary; it is possible under this schema for settler Canadians to keep indigenous peoples as radically Other.[8] The dispute over Musqueam Park, however, confounds these concepts because, within the confines of the Canadian legal system and its accompanying ideologies of capitalism and equality, the Band's claims were not different or incommensurable. The Band was doing what the Canadian state, through legislation like the *Indian Act*, had legally prevented it from doing for years: attempting to maximize the profitability of prime real estate in West Vancouver based on favorable market conditions. Within Canadian capitalist logic, the Band's raising of rents was reasonable, legal, and lucrative. It was, as Chief Ernest Campbell characterized it, "a private business arrangement with our tenants."[9] Describing the dispute in this way confounds the notion of the Musqueam as radically Other and shuts down the discursive opportunity for the leaseholders to object to Musqueam claims on the basis of liberal-democratic ideals. Thus the commensurability of the Musqueam claim required that the leaseholders and other settler Canadians express their opposition in a different way. They evoked an oppositional discourse of difference, attempting to re-inscribe reserve land as "Indian land" with profound material effects. Further, they used this discourse to focus on the ability, and indeed desirability, of indigenous peoples to conduct business in Canada. Finally, leaseholders appropriated languages of oppression including comparisons of their situation to apartheid, ethnic cleansing and colonialism in order to mediate between the seemingly irreconcilable representations of the Musqueam Band as landlords and the Musqueam Band as "Indians."

Several months prior to the Supreme Court's decision, the Canadian edition of *Time Magazine* ran a cover story entitled "The Struggle Over Native Rights," asserting that "flash points of irritation and hostility are erupting as non-natives struggle to come to terms with the most sweeping and comprehensive social adjustment in the country's history: the attempt to bring justice and closure to the frustrated claims of aboriginal peoples" (Frank 2000:18). Although the text only featured a brief discussion of the Musqueam Park dispute, the second-largest photograph in the article featured one of the leaseholders, Kerry-Lynne Findlay, as she stood protectively holding her two young children. The photo spans two pages, and as they stand under a tree on their well-groomed leasehold with their house in the background, the caption reads: "Stuck:Kerry-Lynne Findlay's land lease went from $450 to $36,000 a year" (Frank 2000:22–23). Next to the photo of Findlay is a smaller photo of Gail Sparrow, the former Chief of the Musqueam Band and a vocal opponent of the Band's position. Sparrow is pictured leaning on a white picket fence in front of her home, and the caption below reads: "Former Chief Gail Sparrow objects to sky-high rent hikes." Across the bottom, spanning two pages and flanked by two arrows, was the following caption: "The Musqueam Indian Band wants 7000% land-rent increases from some resentful homeowners." Except for Sparrow, no one else from the Band is quoted or pictured in this article.

A closer examination of these images can reveal some of the popular discourses surrounding the dispute. In *Time*'s configuration, the dispute in Musqueam Park is framed as an indigenous rights issue rather than a civil dispute over property. The leaseholders are described as "homeowners," and the specific legal claims of the Band are not well-defined.[10] As part of "The Struggle Over Native Rights," Findlay and the other leaseholders are presented as iconic of what could happen to "ordinary Canadians" if the pendulum of "social adjustment" were to shift too far in the other direction.

The piece also features two very important settler symbols of property: the home and the fence. The article's description of the leaseholders as "homeowners" rather than "tenants" firmly situates them as differently entitled and deserving of protection. This sense of a threat to home ownership is reinforced by Findlay's statement on the preceding page: "Most people look on their homes as a sanctuary from the world. We'll never feel comfortable here again" (Frank 2000:21). By deploying powerful symbols of home and ownership, Findlay demonstrates that the leaseholders experienced not only a material threat, but a symbolic one. Further, by making claims in the name of "most people," Findlay appeals to a wider sense of entitlement and translates the monetary dispute over rent to a threat to Canadian homeownership in general.

Sparrow's support for the leaseholders was widely reported, and she became a prominent symbol of the Band's unreasonableness. In placing her on a white picket fence, *Time Magazine* visually represented Sparrow as part of a particular property regime with clear boundaries defined by recognizable symbols of ownership. Patricia Seed's historical account of the importance of fences in English claims to land offers a way to read this picture:

To Englishmen . . . fences terminated the rights of communal land-holders. Thus, laying out boundaries, building stone walls, and putting up hedges created the reliable sensation of familiarity and rightness among English colonists dispossessing "communal" Indian landowners in the New World (2001:39).

Time associates Sparrow with those fences that "terminated the rights of communal landholders" (the Musqueam Band), specifically with the symbol of the "white picket fence" and its connotations of home and safety.

BC Report, a conservative newsmagazine, published an article entitled "Circling the wagons: Musqueam leaseholders refuse to pay crippling rate increases and look to Ottawa for relief."[11] "Circling the wagons" evokes images of confrontations between pioneers and Indians on the frontier. Such language was common in more conservative news media, and can be read as part of what Furniss has called the "frontier complex": a form of historical epistemology "that provides a certain set of rules and assumptions that guide how 'truths' about the past, and by extension the present, are to be created, understood, and conveyed" (1999:17). In this instance, the Musqueam Park dispute is interpreted through the myth of the frontier, revealing historical continuities between the colonial and the postcolonial. The leaseholders (settlers) are making their "last stand" against the Musqueam Band (Indians) in this contemporary battle, staking a claim and finding solidarity as non-Natives, and looking to the (colonial) government for aid. *BC Report* constructs the leaseholders as a moral force, not only battling hostile attacks from savages, but also forced to rely on the whims of a faraway colonial government.

The leaseholders appealed to this anxiety over a distant and uncaring colonial government. Contending that the federal government had abandoned them, they organized protests, waving placards that read, "Government of Canada has betrayed non-natives on Crown land. Shame on them."[12] They demanded a government buy-out which would have compensated them, not only for the fee simple value of the homes they owned, but also for a portion of the land value.

When the Band attempted to enforce a legally binding agreement, signed by the leaseholders, the leaseholders asserted "indigenous difference": the land was not like any other land, and the Band could not be treated as any other landlord. The Band's claims were simultaneously constructed by settler Canadians as morally unjust as well as economically unsound.

The non-native Musqueam Park residents who built their homes and signed a 99-year lease are trapped. The band has demanded inappropriately high levies for the land. Yet in today's market the homes are no longer sellable, insurable or useful as equity. Would you wish to conduct business in this environment? Is this good for any Canadians, whether native or non-native? Is the Musqueam impasse the flagship for future business operations with natives?[13]

This appeal to the rhetoric of market forces made a clear connection between the "demands" of the Band and the lack of marketability of Musqueam Park homes. It continued to naturalize the argument that the Band and its "punitive" rents were solely responsible, suggesting that the Band's attempts to work within a capitalist system had failed dismally. The leaseholders and their supporters argued that Musqueam Park, as Indian land, is incommensurable with Canadian capitalism; its uncertainties are different than the usual uncertainties inhering in real estate. This discourse moves to keep reserve land, and the Musqueam Band, *out* of the market, *out* of the private sphere of capitalism.

That the leaseholders, and other settler Canadians, have a material stake in keeping Musqueam Park as "Indian" land is obvious, but there is another, more symbolic, issue at stake. Settler culture has a deep ideological commitment to the idea that First Nations are radically Other, a commitment that enables a naturalization of the status quo by seeing differences as purely "cultural" and dislocated from any historical, political or material context. First Nations marginalization from the benefits of capitalism is a complex issue, but a popular conception is that it is incommensurable with their "culture."[14] Through this kind of reading, Canadian settler culture simultaneously reaps the material benefits of this marginalization *and* conceives of itself as non-violent, non-racist and benevolent.[15] The Musqueam claim, however, unsettles this ideology by confounding notions of cultural incommensurability.

The leaseholders and their supporters counter the Musqueam claim not by the usual appeal to liberal-democratic ideals of equality or sameness, but rather by appealing to powerful moral discourses of oppression. By constructing themselves as victims of apartheid, ethnic cleansing and colonialism, the leaseholders simultaneously assert their innocence and construct the Band's claims (and the Band itself) as morally bankrupt.

Appealing to the values of an ostensibly politically and culturally neutral multiculturalism (see e.g., Mackey 1999), settler Canadians accused the Musqueam of defining themselves and their interests through the non-transcendent and taboo category of "race." Another *Vancouver Sun* editorial responded to the dispute by writing, "Ahead . . . lie infinite down-and-dirty scrambles for land, money and other compensation by aboriginals whose claims rest on race, family, clan, 'purity' of Indian/tribal blood, and so on."[16]

Characterizing race as a naturalized category, created by First Nations, again elides the history of colonial policies like the imposition of Canada's *Indian Act*. Canada has been throughout its existence explicitly concerned with defining who is and is not "Indian," and with separating, physically and materially, legally and ideologically, actual "Indians" from "ordinary Canadians." The effects of these separations, including the expropriation of Aboriginal territories, the use of Aboriginal peoples as wage laborers for colonial capitalist expansion, the creation of reserves, the imposition of colonial legal systems, and the persistent and pervasive negative stereotyping of Aboriginal peoples as noble savages or child-like drunks, are constitutive of the current marginalization that Aboriginal peoples experience in BC and Canada more generally. As Razack argues, "The forgetting or disavowal of bodies of colour in the national story secures specific material arrangements and simultaneously shapes dominant subjects' understanding of themselves as entitled and good" (1999:174).

In her discussion of Canadian multiculturalism and its reliance on "difference" to create a national identity of "pluralism, diversity and tolerance," scholar Eva Mackey asks how those differences perceived to be "dangerous" or "threatening" are "contained, controlled, normalised, stereotyped, idealised, marginalised, and reified" (1999:5–6). Musqueam Park leaseholders responded to perceived threats against their privilege by appropriating powerful symbols of racial oppression and recreating themselves as *different*, as "marginalized." But again, as "ordinary Canadians," as "nonnatives," they create their marginalization and yet maintain the privilege of always invisible "whiteness" in contrast to the very visible racialization of the Musqueam in particular and Indians more generally.[17] By marking the Musqueam Band as "Indians" and the leaseholders as "ordinary Canadians," settler discourse reinscribes *race* on First Nations, simultaneously reinforcing extant racism and hostility towards them and constructing the leaseholders as victims of marginalization.

Common statements such as "The roots of the controversy reach back to 1965," and "You can't make up for years of injustice on the backs of 74 residents" place the dispute in a particular spatial and temporal configuration, limiting the relevance of colonialism and attempting to write the indigenous/settler experience as something distant and devoid of context.[18]

> They have lived on the land for many years. They are being forced to leave by a series of duplicitous legal manoeuvers [sic]. And they have no recourse through the political system. The plight of the Musqueam Park residents sounds rather like most native groups' tales of their own experiences during the settlement of early Canada. And yet those forcing the residents off their land are not nasty colonial settlers, but a native band council.[19]

The replacement of "nasty colonial settlers" with "native band council," an ironic inversion of the usual players, retells a history of colonialism as a phenomenon long past, without any contemporary relevance to indigenous or settler Canadians. Colonial violence and its effects are temporally distanced, part of "the settlement of early Canada," suggesting that they do not persist in Canada's current liberal democratic incarnation. Further, this passage appropriates the language of colonial oppression, thus *re*historicizing the perceived victimization of the leaseholders. By using narratives "rather like most native groups' tales of their experiences," settler discourse asserts its innocence in the face of First Nations' challenges to its legitimacy.

In this same editorial, the *Post* argues that the Musqueam Park dispute has resulted in "Fiscal cleansing in BC." It contended that should the Band win the Supreme Court decision, "the result will be the effective expropriation of property and deliberate de-population of Musqueam Park."[20] This rhetoric was picked up by the leaseholders during a protest of Indian affairs minister Robert Nault when they sported t-shirts saying "Victims of Fiscal Cleansing."[21]

Statements like "It's apartheid. It smacks of the same kinds of injustices . . ."[22] and "The new apartheid: what happens when the job of racially partitioning Canada through the land claims process is complete?"[23] were pervasive, both in the Musqueam Park dispute and in others involving encounters between settlers and First Nations (e.g., Bateman 1997; Tennant 1990). Apartheid, ethnic cleansing and colonialism, powerful moral symbols of discrimination and oppression, are removed from their violent, historically-specific contexts in order maximize the rhetorical strength of the leaseholders' claims. Any sustained comparison of the actual conditions of apartheid, ethnic cleansing or colonialism with the conditions in Musqueam Park would be absurd. Why, then, was this strategy of "oppression" so ubiquitous in settler discourse, and why was it so effective in asserting a sympathetic claim for the leaseholders?

The radical decontextualization that occurs in these juxtapositions is important to settler discourse because it relies on the *symbolism* of oppression as opposed to any lived experience of it. This creates a double movement. First, the leaseholders claim a quasi-indigenous identity (as oppressed) in order to create sympathy and to demand a remedy for their situation.[24] Second, a symbolic claim to oppression can also work to diminish the force of the other legitimate claims, and these kinds of equations can have a neutralizing effect. Leaseholder discourse, then, mediates the *unsettling* of Musqueam Park, articulating its own marginalization by marking the racial difference of "Indians" against the invisibility of "whiteness" and by evoking the symbolism of oppression. This ideological attempt at a *re*-settlement of Musqueam Park appropriates the language of oppression while reinscribing the "unspeakable" racism that exists against First Nations in Canada.

Through its deployment of laden and dichotomous categories such as "native/non-native" and "native/ordinary Canadian," leaseholder discourse further reveals a racialized interest in law and property. By evoking certain forms of whiteness, especially those that preclude any explicit discussion of race, with the effect of effacing its very existence, leaseholder discourse intersects with Canadian law, working in tandem to secure the symbolic and material conditions needed for a twenty-first century resettlement of Musqueam Park.

WHEN THE EXCLUDED RE-ENTERS: PROPERTY
AND DIFFERENCE IN A SETTLER SOCIETY

> In ascribing what is excluded to the colonized, peasants, and other
> incommensurables, not only must their difference to what emerges be
> fabricated and asserted but also their similarity to what is within must
> be denied [Fitzpatrick 1999:55].

In attempting to redress both the historic and contemporary injustices
wrought by colonialism, indigenous peoples in Canada and throughout the
world have sought legal remedies in settler courts. A wide body of literature has demonstrated the serious limitations placed on indigenous peoples
when they are required to articulate their claims in the institutions and
languages of their colonizers.[25] These works analyze the complex terrain of
law and its relationship to postcolonialism, demonstrating how epistemologically distinct claims made by indigenous peoples have been managed by
settler courts. This literature further examines the evocation of difference
in legal cases involving indigenous peoples, especially the use of difference
as critique. In this sense, indigenous claims are used to defamiliarize the
familiar, and to point out some of law's fundamental assumptions.

Yet these types of analyses cannot account for what happened in Musqueam Park. The Band did not make its claims through the idiom of
indigenous difference, but rather through attempted participation in the
private sphere of Canadian capitalism. In contrast, it was the leaseholders who made self-consciously cultural (*qua* racial) assertions. Ironically,
the dominant rhetoric of opposition to indigenous claims in Canada usually operates "by emphasizing the liberal-democratic ideals of individualism, private property, and equality for all" (Bateman 1997:61). In this
instance, however, the Band's claims were commensurable with these
liberal-democratic ideals.

The Band's commensurable claims confound notions of indigenous difference, notions that are central both to settler identity and to associated
concepts of property. This commensurability was deeply unsettling to the
leaseholders and other settler Canadians. In his discussion of the concept
of discovery in law, Fitzpatrick explores the legal construction of difference
and offers a way to read the dispute in Musqueam Park:

> This construction [of an Other] involves that which is acceptable or
> within the identity being created in its difference to that which is unfit
> and excluded. Looked at in reverse, if the excluded were to reenter, as
> it were, then the identity would disintegrate . . . (1999:55).

To reformulate Fitzpatrick's insight: it is not *if* the excluded re-enters, but
rather *when* the excluded, in this case the Musqueam Band, re-enters. Indigenous peoples have traditionally been excluded from the liberal-democratic

spheres of "individualism, private property, and equality for all," an exclusion which allowed settler identities to be forged in opposition. The Band "re-enters" when it asserts its entrepreneurial desires and demands a legal remedy in line with common law real estate practice.

In his discussion of mainstream legal responses to indigenous claims about "culture loss," anthropologist Stuart Kirsch argues that a profound limitation of Anglo-American property regimes, especially in terms of appreciating the diverse and complex property regimes of indigenous peoples throughout the world, is "the assumption of alienability—the view that all forms of property are inherently convertible into other forms of property" (2001:176). Yet an ironic inversion of this assumption of alienability is expressed in the *Glass* decision; the majority Court found that because *leasehold reserve land* is not alienable in the same sense as freehold land, Musqueam Park is considered to be outside of the regular ambit of the market even for the purposes of calculating leasehold rents. It is precisely its definition as inalienable and as communally owned that provides legal justification for the Court to deny the Band's claim of commensurability under the law. Thus, colonial legal categories of collective ownership, inalienability of land, and the idea of Aboriginal title are presumed to be essential categories inhering in the land itself and are used to legitimize the rent discounts in Musqueam Park. The effacement of this colonial history was not merely incidental to the Supreme Court's decision, but rather constitutive of it.

LOOKING THROUGH *GLASS*:
THE VALUE OF INDIAN LAND

Through an analysis of court decisions, I will now explore what Sarah Jain calls "the category work of legal forums" (2004:70), examining the ways in which Canadian courts work to normalize and legitimize settler claims to Musqueam Park. I will focus on the discursive dimensions of *Glass*, exploring how legal discourse ultimately constructs Musqueam Park as fundamentally different and inimical to profit-making. Despite the seemingly progressive nature of recent decisions recognizing Aboriginal title (e.g., *Delgamuukw* in Canada and *Mabo* in Australia), the Supreme Court's decision in *Glass* demonstrates a novel set of limitations inhering in European legal categories; namely, the arguments that produce decisions recognizing Aboriginal title are the very same arguments that severely limit what the Musqueam and other First Nations can do with reserve land. Most interesting is the way in which categories are deployed in the deeply politicized context of Musqueam Park dispute. The application of legal concepts such as inalienability in order to create a *sui generis* category of property, *leasehold reserve land*, becomes part of an essentialist legal discourse that works to devalue Indian land, and simultaneously to legitimize leaseholder claims to that same land.

FEDERAL COURT OF CANADA (TRIAL DIVISION)

> The evidence amply supports the proposition that land on the Musqueam Reserve may be expected to have a lower value than neighbouring fee simple land. The factors affecting land value on the Musqueam Reserve do not constitute the imposition of artificial or discriminatory considerations by this Court. The appraisers and real estate agent who have testified have observed that *the marketplace values leased Indian reserve land at less than fee simple land and have provided substantive reasons, which happen to be linked to the nature of that land, as to why this occurs* [*Musqueam Indian Band v. Glass*, (1997), [1998] 1 F.C. D-34; my emphasis].

In 1997, the Federal Court of Canada (FCC) heard *Musqueam Indian Band v. Glass* in order to determine the meaning of "fair rent" and "current land value" as stated in the leases. In this case, the Band argued that the lots in Musqueam Park should be valued as though "for sale in the real estate market, *i.e.* [for] their fee simple value" (1997). It asserted that Musqueam Park assessments should be based on the value of other nearby freehold lots in southwest Vancouver, and its appraisers estimated the average value of the unimproved land in Musqueam Park to be between $600,000 and $700,000 per lot. Conversely, the leaseholders argued that the land should be "valued on the basis of a leasehold interest in land on an Indian reserve," and their appraiser estimated the average lot to be worth only $132,000 (1997).

In his decision, Judge Marshall Rothstein sided with the leaseholders, concluding that the value of the land could not be determined as though it were freehold. Rothstein ruled that Musqueam Park lots are "unique" because they are part of an Indian Reserve, and thus subject to "uncertainties related to property taxation, native self government, servicing and other matters" (1997). Citing reasons such as "the Indians' jurisdiction over the land," "the publicized unrest" on Indian reserves in BC,[26] and the inability for non-Indian residents to participate in Band government, the judge asserted that "it is clear that the leasehold and Indian Reserve aspects had a significant negative influence on the marketability and value of the property" (1997). He accepted the leaseholders' appraisal and concluded that "current land value" for the Musqueam Park lots should be fifty percent of the fee simple value less the value of improvements, resulting in an average rent per lot per year of $10,000.

One might assume that Rothstein made a distinction between Musqueam Park and other adjacent fee simple settlements based on the idea that *leasehold* land, as land with a particular kind of encumbrance, is inherently less valuable than freehold land; however, he ruled that "there is no material difference" between them. Rather, according to Rothstein, the "material difference" in the value of the lots in Musqueam

Park comes from "the nature of [Indian] land" (1997). Rothstein held that because of its legal circumscription as land that is held collectively and is inalienable, reserve land cannot be considered analogous to freehold land. There are two key issues with Rothstein's argument. First, rarely are appraisals for calculating leasehold rents based on the actual sale of the property; instead, they are usually hypothetical appraisals reflecting what the land could be sold for in the open market given current conditions. Second, Rothstein's determination that "Indian land" is fundamentally different is in no way based on how the land was being valued *prior* to 1995. As Armstrong (2000) points out, Musqueam Park properties were being valued and sold at prices comparable to similarly situated freehold properties, and as I noted earlier, the bulk of that value adhered to the leaseholders in the form of property values. Yet, the Band's attempt to realign the distribution of wealth inhering in Musqueam Park through participation in common law real estate practice is legally and publicly reinterpreted as "uncertainty," resulting in a depression of property values.

FEDERAL COURT OF APPEAL

The Band appealed Rothstein's initial decision to the Federal Court of Appeal (FCA) in 1998. In stark contrast to Judge Rothstein, the three-judge panel accepted the Band's claims and overturned Rothstein's decision, asserting that the land should be treated as fee simple land for the purposes of determining its current value [*Musqueam Indian Band v. Glass*, 1998 CanLII 9036 (F.C.A.)]. The panel further maintained that the reference to "current land value" in the original lease was intended to mean the fee simple value of the land. The panel held that the trial court had erred in its determination that the land should be discounted by fifty percent. The panel reacted to what it saw as a discriminatory decision by Rothstein, arguing that "there is no authority for taking into account the identity of the owner in the determination of the land value. Aboriginal land should not be treated differently from other land" (1998).

SUPREME COURT OF CANADA

> Moreover, as a safeguard and protection to these Indian Communities, who might, in their primal state of ignorance and natural improvidence, have made away with the land, it was provided that these Reserves should be the common property of the Tribe, and that the title should remain vested in the Crown, so as to be inalienable by any of their own acts. . . .

Letter from BC Governor James Douglas to Indian Superintendent
I.W. Powell, 1874 [cited in Harris 2002:44]

The hypothetical used to establish market value in the absence of an
actual market should reflect the land as it is in its actual circumstances
and should not change the nature of the land appraised. Since it has
chosen not to surrender the land for sale, the Band holds reserve land
and must accept the realities of the market for this capital asset.
[Supreme Court of Canada, majority decision, *Musqueam Indian
Band v. Glass*, 2000]

Carol Rose argues that claims to ownership must be understood as culturally specific narratives in which "the would-be 'possessor' has to send a
message that others in the culture understand and that they find persuasive
as grounds for the claim asserted" (1994:25). The controversy surrounding
Musqueam Park and the Court's ultimate decision in *Glass* demonstrate
that the Band's claim, articulated in a capitalist idiom of private property
and equality, was not especially persuasive in the cultural context of settler Canada. But why were the Band's commensurable claims unsuccessful?
And further, what is "the nature of Indian land," and why is it less valuable
than other forms of property?

A key legal question was how "Indian land" should be understood in the
specific context of assessing its hypothetical value for the purpose of calculating annual leasehold rents. According to the Supreme Court's majority
decision in *Glass*, the inalienability of reserve land was an important factor
in appraising its value, and the Band's "choice" not to surrender the land
for sale ultimately lessened its worth. But why were the inalienability and
collective nature of reserve land relevant to this kind of appraisal?

The two quotations cited above point to some of the contradictions inhering
in legal discourses about reserve land. The first is representative of nineteenth
century paternalistic policies created by colonial governments to "protect"
the small tracts of land reserved for indigenous peoples from unscrupulous
settlers. Features such as the inalienability of reserve land and the collective
nature of Indian ownership emerge directly out of these policies. The second
demonstrates how these earlier policies have been translated into contemporary legal discourse: the "actual circumstances," "the nature of the land," and
the "realities of the market" limit what the Band can do with its land while
making the land more accessible and valuable to settler Canadians.

In overturning the appeals court decision, the Supreme Court majority
accepted leaseholder assertions that *leasehold reserve land* constitutes a *sui
generis* legal category:

The words "current land value" must be interpreted as referring to the
value of the actual land comprised in the leases, namely land held in

aboriginal title in a reserve by a Band that has not surrendered all its rights and interest in the land *but has retained them* and not the value of land held in freehold title outside a reserve in which the Band has no rights or interest [Appellants' Factum 2000:20].

Several contradictions emerge in this discourse. First, although the reserve has been inscribed in particular ways that both create and severely limit the Band's choices, neither these limitations nor their origins are explored in the decision. It is not simply that the Court has effaced these dimensions in an attempt to sufficiently narrow its scope; rather, its decision to discount rents in Musqueam Park would be impossible without this effacement.

Second, the Supreme Court's majority sets up an ironic situation in which the Band, by maintaining its land base (usually considered an essential element of First Nations cultural and financial well-being), faces serious economic loss. The choice articulated in the Court's majority decision is basically this: surrender the reserve to the Crown or suffer the economic consequences of holding (leasehold) reserve land. Either way, the Musqueam Band is legally prevented from participation in free market capitalism.

Third, if the Band *were* to unconditionally surrender its land for sale, would it not be the case that after surrender it would be ineligible to collect on the leases, thus making the entire dispute a moot point? As Chief Justice McLachlin (dissenting) asserted:

> The proposed 50 percent reduction for reserve related factors depends on the valuation of an interest that could simply never exist. As the trial court noted, reserve land can be converted to fee simple only by surrender to the Crown. Once reserve land is surrendered to the Crown, it loses all the characteristics of reserve land. Thus there can be no such thing as fee simple title to reserve land. *Given that no such interest can ever exist, it is difficult to see how it could be valued in any principled way* [Glass, 9].

If one follows the majority Court's logic, then the only way it would accept the Band's appraisal of Musqueam Park would be if the Band no longer held title to it. Thus, the majority decision rests on the evocation of specific (and logically impossible) circumstances to justify a hypothetical appraisal, an appraisal that must necessarily be seen as deeply politicized given the controversy surrounding it.

Thus, in *Glass*, the profound political and cultural implications of the Band's decision *not* to surrender its land to the Crown, couched in the legal language of rationality and choice, have been completely effaced. The issue then becomes whether or not the Band prefers to maintain its only legally guaranteed land base; if so, according to the Court, it must then accept the political and economic consequences.

CONCLUSION: RESETTLING MUSQUEAM PARK

On its surface, the dispute over Musqueam Park seemed to be a rather routine one about leases, rents, and real estate, yet a deeper analysis reveals not only the centrality of property in the organization of settler imaginaries but also how terms of cultural difference operate in novel and unexpected ways at this historical moment. Through appeal to colonial legal categories like inalienability, collective ownership, and Aboriginal title, the courts constructed "Indian land" as fundamentally different from other forms of property. Further, by rendering certain relevant colonial historical relationships invisible, they created a *sui generis* form of property—*leasehold reserve land*—that effectively prevented the Musqueam Band from full (and profitable) participation in Vancouver's booming housing market. In this sense, legal discourses of difference and indigeneity work to *resettle* Musqueam Park both by limiting the Band's ability to profit and by enabling a significant part of the value of 'Indian land' to accrue to the settler Canadians leasing it.

Amidst an intense public battle fought in the courts, the political arena, and the press, leaseholders attempted to stake a claim to Musqueam Park, arguing that what they saw as the Band's attempt to displace them from the land and their homes was both morally suspect and economically unviable. Leaseholders responded to potential dislocation by using deeply racialized rhetoric, analogizing their situation to colonialism, apartheid, and ethnic cleansing.

Ideas of property and ownership not only structure Canadian legal and economic systems, but also are central cultural metaphors through which citizens articulate entitlement and belonging. The Musqueam Band's commensurable legal claims and attempt to profit from a capital investment provoked widespread controversy among settler Canadians, especially in BC. Despite the seeming novelty of the Band's claim to commensurability, its reception in the courts resulted in the legal encoding of much more familiar settler relations in the province:

> Colonialism and colonization were about the control of land; land use itself defined new rights, exclusions, and patterns of dominance; and strategies for the effective control of land operationalized colonial rhetorics and discourses (Harris 1997:185).

Cole Harris's description of what he calls the first (nineteenth century) resettlement of British Columbia provides us with a framework to understand how legal discourse, culminating in the Supreme Court's decision in *Glass*, works to define "new rights, exclusions, and patterns of dominance" in the legal environment of the twenty-first century. While fostered in the context of a national commitment to multiculturalism and recognition of indigeneity, the legal encoding of difference nevertheless operates in neocolonial ways to further dispossess indigenous peoples of control over their land and of income.

While the official version of the Canadian national anthem begins, "O Canada, our home *and* native land," another version has circulated widely as a critical reminder of longstanding indigenous claims. This other arrangement, "O Canada, our home *on* native land," challenges the legitimacy of European settlement and claims to ownership. While this newer formulation has, of course, been hotly contested, it nevertheless points us to a key element in this dispute. In Musqueam Park, the leaseholders literally make their homes *on* what the government legally categorizes as "Indian land." The Musqueam Park leaseholders are by no means unique in BC, and they represent a growing trend.[27]

What distinguished *Glass* from many cases is that the Indians involved articulated their claim in the legal idiom of Canadian capitalism, attempting to maximize profit on an investment through the application of common law real estate practice. While the outcome of this case was structured by the specific historical, legal, and political landscapes of BC and Canada, it can nevertheless offer a point of departure for a more general discussion about the nature and reception of indigenous claims throughout the world in the late twentieth and early twenty-first centuries, especially in former British colonies where issues involving land and property are paramount. As indigenous peoples continue to participate in the realm of capitalist enterprise, and as their lives are increasingly ordered by the vagaries of late capitalism, how they are legally allowed to function in this realm becomes increasingly important.

5 Of Caucasoids and Kin
Kennewick Man, Race, and Genetic Indigeneity in *Bonnichsen v. United States*

DNA Enters Dust Up Over Bones
A 9300-year-old skeleton uncovered on the banks of the Columbia River in Washington State is a treasure trove of information for
anthropologists, with a projectile point in its pelvis and possible Caucasoid features. But American Indians are claiming the skeleton as an
ancestor and plan to rebury it. However, a sliver of bone taken for
age-testing may soon yield DNA, which may reveal whether the skeleton was ancestral to modern American Indians [Gibbons 1996:172].

INTRODUCTION: KENNEWICK MAN—THE ANCIENT ONE

I begin this chapter with the oft-repeated tale of the 1996 discovery of
human remains in Washington State. At the end of July that year, two
young men inadvertently discovered a human skull while walking along
the banks of the Columbia River near Kennewick, Washington. They noti-
fied local authorities who, after a more thorough search, found not only a
skull but also an almost complete human skeleton. A preliminary police
investigation determined that the remains were not those of a recent victim,
but rather of someone who had lived and died well before the end of the
twentieth century. Dr. James Chatters and other consulting archaeologists
first posited that the remains were those of a nineteenth century European
male settler, but the later discovery of a projectile point embedded in the
hip suggested otherwise (Chatters 2001). Preliminary carbon-dating tests
put the age of the remains at approximately 9200 years old, making the
"Kennewick Man," as he was eventually dubbed by archaeologists and the
media, among the earliest and most complete human skeletons ever found
in North America.

By September 1996, the first of several controversies concerning the
proper disposition of the remains emerged. Federal legislation, the Native
American Graves Protection and Repatriation Act of 1990 (NAGPRA),
recognized the right of American Indian tribes to have Native American
remains and other cultural objects found on federal or tribal lands repatriated.[1] Based on the age of the skeleton and the location in which it was

discovered, a coalition of five local tribes appealed to the federal government and asked that the remains of Kennewick Man—whom the tribes called the Ancient One—be returned to them for immediate reburial in concert with their religious and cultural values.[2] The tribal coalition maintained that Kennewick Man was an ancestor and that jurisdiction over his remains belonged to them under the rules of NAGPRA (Minthorn 1996). A group of archaeologists and physical anthropologists challenged the tribes' claim to the remains, asserting that any reburial of Kennewick Man prior to a careful scientific investigation would be a profound loss not only to science but also to humanity as a whole.[3] Further, the scientists contested the position that the remains were unequivocally "Native American" and could be easily linked to any of the five contemporary tribes. They suggested instead that Kennewick Man's morphology—especially his "Caucasoid" or "European" features—pointed to a possibly *pre*-indigenous peopling of the Americas.[4] This latter contention, and its accompanying racial idiom, was picked up by the media and was widely circulated in news pieces such as "Old Skull Gets White Looks" and "Is Kennewick Man 'Asian' or 'European'?"[5]

In late 1996, the federal government, more specifically the Army Corps of Engineers, concurred with the tribal coalition that Kennewick Man was Native American under the NAGPRA statute and ordered the remains repatriated to the tribes for reburial without further scientific study. A group of eight plaintiff-scientists, led by anthropologist Robson Bonnichsen, challenged the ruling by filing suit in federal court (*Bonnichsen v. United States*).[6] What followed over the ensuing eight years brought a series of issues into stark relief, including the rights of indigenous peoples under US law, the role of scientific conceptions of race and history, and the legitimacy and efficacy of NAGPRA. The question of what and who Kennewick Man was, and to whom he belonged, sparked a series of legal battles that continued for nearly a decade.[7]

The key legal issues in the *Bonnichsen* litigation hinged on whether or not the remains of Kennewick Man are in fact "Native American" as defined in NAGPRA. In 2004, the Ninth Circuit Court of Appeals upheld an earlier district court ruling that Kennewick Man did not fit the category of "Native American": "Human remains that are 8340 to 9200 years old and that bear only incidental genetic resemblance to modern-day American Indians, along with incidental genetic resemblance to other peoples, cannot be said to be the Indians' 'ancestors' within Congress's meaning" (*Bonnichsen IV*:5072).

Much has been written about the legal battles surrounding the remains.[8] This chapter is not so much a commentary on the legal disposition of Kennewick Man, but rather a discussion of the *Bonnichsen* court's legal decisions as they relate to ideas of genetics, indigeneity, and identity at the beginning of the twenty-first century. I provide a critical reading of documents—of evidentiary claims, scientific reports, legal analyses, and media accounts—in order to assess the simultaneous assertions and denials of indigeneity in the context of this case. More specifically, I explore the legal importance of "biological ancestry"—frequently constructed in the idioms of race and genetics—in establishing whether or not the remains of Kennewick Man could be linked to "a *presently existing* tribe, people, or culture to be considered Native American" (*Bonnichsen IV*; emphasis in original). What does it mean that human remains thought to be at least nine thousand years old, and thus clearly "pre-Columbian," do not legally qualify as "Native American" in US courts? What does it mean to use "genetic resemblance" (or the absence thereof) as a legal marker of identity when no viable DNA was recovered from the remains of Kennewick Man? To answer these questions, I trace what I call *genetic indigeneity* as a marker of a discursive shift from a public, scientific, and legal understanding of indigeneity whose predominant metaphor is blood to one in which the predominant metaphor is genes. In the *Bonnichsen* decisions, the genetic becomes the proving ground of indigeneity and articulates with ideas of racial and morphological difference. As issues of race, ethnicity, and indigeneity are becoming newly entangled with contemporary ideas of the genetic (e.g., TallBear 2003, 2007), how are long-circulating idioms of racial science marshaled and reinvigorated in discourses of genetics?

INDIAN LEGAL IDENTITY

The legal history of Indian identity in the United States is both complex and contradictory. "Who is an Indian?" has been a key question in the United States since the mid-nineteenth century, one deeply bound to processes of Euro-American colonization (e.g., Brownell 2001; Meyer 1999:234). While this question is not an exclusively legal one, it has nevertheless dominated issues of federal Indian law. At various times throughout US legal history, establishing who is and is not Indian has been central to determining collective and individual identities. These identities are, in turn, tied to questions of land and resource distribution, property, inheritance, treaty payments, state and federal benefits, civil and criminal jurisdiction, tribal membership, and political rights (e.g., Biolsi 2001; Kauanui 2002; Ray 2006; Rohrer 2006; Sturm 2002; Turner Strong and Van Winkle 1996). The legal disposition of the remains of Kennewick Man introduces another dimension to the question of Indian identity at the turn of the twenty-first century. In the following sections, I offer a brief historical perspective on repatriation and anthropology in order to contextualize some of the terms and ideas circulating in the dispute over Kennewick Man. The debate over Kennewick Man and the meaning of "Native American" as articulated in the *Bonnichsen* litigation becomes another chapter in the long history of the question "Who is an Indian?" What marks this as especially important

is the emergence of *genetic indigeneity*—even in the absence of genetics—
as a key evidentiary marker of identity.

Arguably one of the most salient aspects of Indian legal identity in the
United States has been, and continues to be, blood quantum. Determination of Indian identity both politically and culturally is often based on
blood quantum, usually a measurement of "how much" of an individual's
"blood" (as a unit of heredity) has been inherited from Indian ancestors.
While concepts of blood quantum have evolved over time, they have nevertheless been consistently associated with extant and emergent ideas of race
in American society (see e.g., Garroutte 2003; Spruhan 2006; Sturm 2002).
Because blood quantum, both in its conceptual and institutional forms, is
so deeply ingrained in understandings of Indian identity, it must be seen as
essential to struggles "for existence, resources, and recognition" (Turner
Strong and Van Winkle 1996:554). In some ways, the legal battle over
the identity of Kennewick Man is but another example of such struggles,
deeply rooted in longstanding colonial legacies. Yet anthropologist Richard
Warren Perry reminds us of "how new technologies have created new pos-
sibilities for the assertion of conflicting blood-and-soil identity claims, and
new rhetorics of racial contestations" (2002:144). My purpose here is to
use the Kennewick Man controversy as a case study in order to sketch some
of the dimensions of these "new rhetorics of racial contestation" especially
as they articulate with emergent idioms of race and genetics.

AMERICAN INDIANS, RACIAL SCIENCE, AND NAGPRA

> Scientific claims to Indian dead have a political and cultural genealogy
> that scientists and their publics cannot be allowed to forget [Dumont
> 2003:124].

The passage of the Native American Graves Protection and Repatriation
Act (NAGPRA) in 1990 marked an important moment in the history of US
federal Indian law. NAGPRA was in response to longstanding critiques on
the part of indigenous groups which challenged the historical and continued
expropriation of American Indian remains and sacred objects.[9] American
Indian remains had long had a status different from the remains of other
groups. While Anglo-American common law has historically protected the
dead and associated funerary objects from pilfering and other forms of
desecration, "it has been commonplace for public agencies to treat Native
American dead as archaeological resources, property, pathological material, data, specimens, or library books, but not as human beings" (Trope
and Echohawk 1998:179). Legal scholar Allison Dussias and others locate
such practices in "the belief that the racial inferiority of Native Americans
condemned them to extinction," thus making "everything that belonged
to Native Americans, from their land to the very bodies of their deceased

family members" available for the taking (2005:72; see also Bieder 1986; LaVaque-Manty 2000; Trigger 1980, 2003).

While in the nearly twenty years since its passage NAGPRA has been the subject of extensive study and commentary (e.g., Hibbert 1998/1999; Mihesuah 2000; Pensley 2005; Riding In et al. 2004; Yasaitis 2005), there are two key points about the legislation necessary for the analysis here. The first is that NAGPRA itself was considered remedial legislation, in part meant to address the historic inequities found in law and in practice; thus, many scholars have suggested that any statutory or evidentiary ambiguities should be decided in favor of tribes (see e.g., Dussias 2005; Harding 2005; Ray 2006; Ripley 2005; Tsosie 1999). The second is that the scientific framework used to evaluate whether or not Kennewick Man was legally "Native American" under NAGPRA ironically emerges from the creation and study of those ill-gotten collections (see Dussias 2005; Highet 2005).[10]

Historian Robert E. Bieder has written extensively about how the collection of American Indian remains was central to the development of experimental practices and modes of inquiry in American anthropology (1986, 1998, 2000).[11] For instance, Samuel Morton, a founding figure in American physical anthropology, believed in the existence of fundamental and measurable biological differences among human groups (see also Dussias 2005; Gould 1996; Lieberman 2001). He was also an empiricist who believed in the necessity of "genuine specimens" (especially crania) to study and to serve as proof of hierarchical taxonomies such as "The Five Races of Man":

> His search for human skulls of all races and his subsequent investigations led not only to the racial findings expressed in his *Crania Americana*, findings that would color racial thinking long after his death in 1851—but also laid the foundation for anthropological interest in the search for deceased Indians . . . (Bieder 1998:164).

Thus, Morton's legacy to physical anthropology was simultaneously conceptual and material. Both his analytical apparatus and his collection practices helped shape the discipline. The legacy of Morton, and of those who followed, is important for contextualizing the kinds of scientific reasoning put forth by the plaintiffs in the *Bonnichsen* litigation, especially in terms of the operation of racialized categories.[12]

There is an extensive critical literature on the historical development of racial science in anthropology, a literature beyond the scope of this chapter.[13] What I wish to recover from these accounts is the centrality (1) of collecting and of comparative evolutionary frameworks, and (2) of racial difference in general, and of indigenous difference in particular, to the conception and practice of physical anthropology (e.g., LaVaque-Manty 2000).[14] While there is nothing in the record to suggest that Chatters or Bonnichsen and the other plaintiffs in any way ally themselves with the clearly racist findings of Morton and other nineteenth century racial scientists, I nevertheless want to make clear the connection between the historical and material conditions through which the disciplines of physical anthropology emerge *and* the racialist assumptions embedded in contemporary forms of analysis.[15] In other words, terms such as "Caucasoid," "Mongoloid," or even "Native American" do not emerge *ex nihilo* but are rather created in, and re-materialized through, historically specific circumstances. Such racialist assumptions not only shape the object of study (the remains of Kennewick Man) and the conditions of that study (the categories and modes of inquiry used to understand the remains) but also set the terms of the legal disposition of the remains. In other words, the question "Who is an Indian?" in the context of NAGPRA is itself is rooted in a variety of nineteenth century legacies in both law and science.

This tension between a foundational racialism that motivates research *and* a self-conscious awareness of the limitations of biological concepts of race is present in other scientific fields including biomedical research and population genetics. In her discussion of race and genomics in the controversial Human Genome Diversity Project (HGDP), Jenny Reardon critiques the prevailing notion that racial science met its demise in the decades following the Second World War:

> Far from marking the decline of racial science and the ascendancy of claims about human equality, subtle differences among statements about the biological meaninglessness of race acted to shore up the power of biological experts and political actors to differentiate humans racially for the purposes of knowing and governing them. Thus, I argue, we should not be surprised when contemporary claims about the biological meaninglessness of race are accompanied by claims about the *meaningfulness* of race, as it is the former that have often enabled the latter (2004:40; emphasis in original).

Assertions of the simultaneous meaningfulness and meaninglessness of biological race were also prevalent in the discourse surrounding the fight over Kennewick Man. In the following example, Chatters discusses his use of the forensic anthropological paradigm:

> Hence, the groupings Mongoloid, Caucasoid, and Negroid should not properly be thought of as races. *The distinctions we impose on our species are therefore arbitrary and have more social import than biological meaning in a taxonomic sense.* The physical differences on which they are based are superficial and, in the words of C. Loring Brace, merely 'kinship writ large.' This does not, however, negate the facts that human populations do differ from one another to some degree and

that those differences, however minor, are an aid to physical identification (2001:173; my emphasis).

Yet, throughout the dispute, Kennewick Man's ostensibly "Caucasoid" features were centrally related to discussions of his ostensible "race" in both legal and extra-legal spheres. The relationships between nineteenth century racial science and contemporary arguments about the existence and importance of Kennewick Man's "Caucasoid" features are not coincidental nor can they be dismissed merely as an inherited nomenclature.[16]

OF CAUCASOIDS AND KIN: OR, WHAT WOULD NATIVE AMERICAN GENETICS LOOK LIKE?

> That biology—at every layer of the onion—is a discourse with a contingent history does not mean that its accounts are matters of 'opinion' or 'merely stories.' It does mean that the material-semiotic tissues are inextricably intermeshed. Discourses are not just words; they are material-semiotic practices through which objects of attention and knowing subjects are both constituted [Haraway 1997:218].

From the beginning, a central part of the public debate surrounding the discovery of Kennewick Man was whether or not the remains were in fact "Caucasian" or "European" as opposed to "Native American."[17] After an initial examination of the skeleton, an examination that relied heavily on morphological categorization, archaeologist James Chatters originally classified Kennewick Man as a nineteenth century European male settler. Although this position became quickly untenable in light of the carbon-dating results, the suggestion that Kennewick Man might be something *other* than Native American had great purchase in both the scientific community and the public imaginary of the late twentieth century United States. As Chatters recounts in his 2001 book, *Ancient Encounters*:

> Kennewick Man was 9,500 years old! *Now* I sat down, my mind flooded with all the ramifications of this outcome. The impact of my understanding of the prehistory of the western United States and the peopling of the Americas was immediate. On a local scale, I had always been taught to expect continuity between the most ancient inhabitants and modern Northwest Indians, yet this man bore no resemblance to the aboriginal peoples of the Columbia River basin. What was this Caucasoid-looking man doing here? Why had conflict—represented by the spear wound—appeared so early in the region's history? On the scale of the hemisphere, the impact was even greater (53; emphasis in original).

Thus, just who Kennewick Man was and to whom he belonged were central questions formulated in terms of "continuity" and "resemblance." From the outset, his identity was vitally linked to questions of race, kinship, and heredity.

In his 2002 monograph, *What It Means to Be 98% Chimpanzee*, biological anthropologist Jonathan Marks argues that in the case of Kennewick Man, "all discussion of descent is metaphorical" (238). More specifically, Marks points out that we have no way of assessing whether or not Kennewick Man had progeny and, as a result, no way of assessing whether or not he could have literal descendants among contemporary peoples. But, of course, tracing the literal descendants of Kennewick Man was not the point of controversy surrounding the remains; rather,

> The issue is the *group* he belonged to, or that we assign him to, and its relationship to today's groups. Scientific or genetic ideas of identity and descent are not the heart of the matter, *for descent is not being taken literally here.* Thus, any claim of ancestry for Kennewick Man is in the realm of folk heredity, in the cultural ideas of relationship among constructed groups. . . . And we have no objective, scientific basis on which to judge one metaphor's validity as against another's. The question of descent from Kennewick Man thus falls outside the domain of science (Marks 2002:238–239; emphasis in original).

Marks' line of reasoning provides a key point of departure from which to discuss the legal disposition of the remains. Part of my task here is to trace how such metaphorical conceptions of descent—of "folk heredity"—are materialized as objective and scientific, especially in terms of genetics, in the realm of the legal (see also Marks 2001a, 2001b). How is it that certain concepts of folk heredity are operationalized in the *Bonnichsen* litigation while others are not?

FORENSIC FACIAL RECONSTRUCTION

> On the physical characteristics alone, he could fit on the streets of Stockholm without causing any kind of notice. Or on the streets of Jerusalem or New Delhi, for that matter. I've been looking around for someone who matches this Kennewick gentleman, looking for weeks and weeks at people on the street, thinking, This one's got a little bit there. And then, one evening, I turned on the TV, and there was Patrick Stewart . . . and I said, "My God, there he is! Kennewick Man!" (James Chatters, cited in Preston 1997:73).

In 1997, using techniques of forensic facial reconstruction, James Chatters joined forces with sculptor Tom McClelland "to help put a face on Kennewick Man."[18] A photo of the Kennewick Man facial reconstruction, first published with an accompanying article in *The New Yorker* in 1998, was picked up by media outlets in the United States and was circulated extensively in print and online.[19] Engendering widespread comparisons to the iconic character of Captain Jean-Luc Picard from the television series, *Star Trek: The Next Generation* (as well as to his portrayer, actor Patrick Stewart), Chatters' and McClelland's model created quite a stir by seeming to visually reinforce the "Caucasoid" origins of Kennewick Man and to actively cultivate what archaeologist Larry Zimmerman calls "a white history for the Americas" (2005:269; see also Crawford 2000).[20] Chatters denied any such intention and wrote of how he was taken aback by the controversy:

> This widely reported comparison elicited an unanticipated reaction. Other media took this statement to mean that I saw Kennewick Man as a European—as a white man. But skulls of course have no skin color. I did not say Kennewick Man looked like a European, but rather that there was a modern European who looked like *him*. I was looking not at skin color but at the face produced by the man's bones. I wanted to do something to let the skull tell its own story (2001:143; emphasis in original).

But what does it mean "to let the skull tell its own story"? In this section, I focus on the forensic facial reconstruction of Kennewick Man and suggest that the methods and practices involved are cultural ones with important implications for how race and relatedness were understood in the context of the *Bonnichsen* decisions.

New Yorker writer Douglas Preston gives the following account of the reconstruction process:

> Chatters and McClelland first stuck little rubber markers onto the cast, indicating the theoretical depth of tissue in various parts of the face. They calculated the shape and size of the nose from nasal bones, and placed eyeballs in the sockets. Then, using clay, they modeled some thirty facial muscles and rolled the skin over them in strips, much like laying down a carpet (1998:52).

Preston's analogy to the relatively mundane practice of "laying down a carpet" belies the intellectual and ideological work that went into creating the model of Kennewick Man's face.[21] As other scholars have demonstrated, scientific methods of representation are themselves cultural practices, necessarily deeply rooted in, and emerging from, the historical, political, and technoscientific contexts in which they are produced (e.g., Lynch and Woolgar 1990).[22] This point is made especially clear when one contrasts the original modeling of Kennewick Man's skull to the more recent (and post-decision) facial representation of Kennewick Man on the cover of *Time Magazine* (Lemonick and Dorfman 2006).[23] In the latter illustration, Kennewick Man looks decidedly unlike anyone who could be classified as "Caucasoid" or "Caucasian"; instead, "[f]ramed by Time magazine's iconic red border, [he] sports dark-hair, a deep tan and an intense-looking gaze."[24]

Donna Haraway's contention that "[b]iology is not the body itself but a discourse on the body" reminds us to pay particular attention to the ways in which cultural understandings of the biological—for instance, our conceptions of race, genetics, and indigeneity—are materialized through discourse (1997:217). Chatters and McClelland had to make various choices about how to represent physical characteristics that simply could not be determined by any existing scientific evidence. The remains of Kennewick Man were skeletal; there was no remaining tissue, hair or viable DNA from which to work. Part of his skull was missing and needed to be reconstructed. Further, in the art and science of forensic facial reconstruction, there are competing schools of thought, and thus no methodological standardization (Reichs 1998). Chatters himself conceded, "No matter how long we might study the Kennewick man we would never know the form or color of his eyes, skin and hair, whether his hair was curly or straight, his lips thin or full—in short many of the characteristics by which we judge living peoples' racial affiliation."[25] Thus, as is necessary in forensic facial reconstruction generally, Chatters and McClelland had to imagine, and to make certain *a priori* assumptions about, the *kind* of human Kennewick Man was. In the politically charged environment of post-NAGPRA battles over ancient human remains, such choices and assumptions articulated with, and provided powerful visual support for, a larger set of claims then circulating in the public sphere, namely, "Is it possible that the first Americans weren't who we think they were?" (Preston 1997:70). Chatters' initial speculation that Kennewick Man possessed morphological features that could be classified as "Caucasoid" fueled even greater speculation about his "Caucasian" origins in the public sphere, and operationalized a rhetoric that worked to render American Indian claims to the remains suspect almost from the outset. Or, to put this rhetoric more bluntly, why should contemporary American Indians have exclusive access to "Caucasoid" human remains when common sense racial categories would suggest that they are themselves part of a different group?

> Kennewick Man, early as he was, was not one of the first Americans. But he could be their descendant. There is evidence that those mysterious first Americans were a Caucasoid people. They may have come from Europe and may be connected to the Clovis people of America. Kennewick may provide evidence of a connection between the Old World and the New (Preston 1997:74).

In Preston's later article about the facial reconstruction, Chatters is quoted as saying, "My responsibility is to make sure he is scientifically and technically correct; Tom's is to give him humanity" (1998:52). But what does it mean to be "scientifically and technically correct" under such conditions? Further, what physical traits come to represent the human in this context? Chatters later wrote, "We gave him no hair or beard and kept the eyes the color of the olive green clay and the skin the gray of the fine plastilina. To choose a hair form or skin color would have been to arbitrarily assign him to some 'race,' which was exactly what we had been so careful to avoid" (2001:147). Yet the visual rhetoric of the "Picard model" of Kennewick Man (a bald head, a pale and hairless face, light eyes except for startling dark pupils, set against a dark background) in tandem with claims to scientific and technical accuracy functions as "an apparatus of capture that makes older traditions of nationalist and racialized discourse seem new again" (Milun 2001:51). At this historical moment, it is difficult to see the widely-circulated Picard model of Kennewick Man as anything other than "white," especially in light of Chatters' explicit comparisons to Patrick Stewart.[26] Further, it is neither accidental nor insignificant that the materialization of Kennewick Man's "humanity" through the practice of forensic facial reconstruction reflects particular racial assumptions, especially about Kennewick Man's phenotypic features. One of Chatters' original conclusions was that Kennewick Man did not look like contemporary American Indian peoples (2000, 2001), a conclusion that is reinforced through the visual apparatus of the model.

In the aforementioned *Time Magazine* article from 2006, the question of Kennewick Man's racial origins was reinvoked: "Was Kennewick Man Caucasian?" Journalists Michael Lemonick and Andrea Dorfman report: "Thanks to Chatters' mention of Caucasoid features back in 1996, the myth that Kennewick Man might have been European never quite died out. The reconstructed skull confirms that he was not—and Chatters never seriously thought otherwise" (2006:49–50).[27] In 2005, artist Tom McClelland cast a series of bronze sculptures from the original mold, one of which is now on display at the Kennewick Library.[28] It is interesting to speculate about how the public may have differently interpreted Kennewick Man and his purported origins had the "bronze-skinned" version been released back in 1998.

BONNICHSEN v. UNITED STATES

As defined in NAGPRA, 'Native American' refers to human remains and cultural items relating to tribes, peoples, or cultures that resided within the area now encompassed by the United States prior to the historically documented arrival of European explorers, irrespective of when a particular group may have begun to reside in this area, and, irrespective of whether some or all of these groups were or were not culturally affiliated or biologically related to present-day Indian tribes

[Memo from Donald J. Barry, Assistant Secretary, Fish and Wildlife and Parks, Department of the Interior, January 2000].

Finally, we address the Secretary's determination that Kennewick Man's remains are Native American, as defined by NAGPRA. We must set aside the Secretary's decision if it was "arbitrary" or "capricious" because the decision was based on inadequate factual support. . . . Here, after reviewing the record, we conclude that the record does not contain substantial evidence that Kennewick Man's remains are Native American within NAGPRA's meaning [*Bonnichsen IV*:5072].

The rest of this chapter is organized around a discussion of what it means to say that human remains dated by contemporary scientific methods as between 8200 and 9300 years old, as clearly "pre-Columbian," do not legally qualify as "Native American" within US courts. I concentrate on the written decisions from the US District Court in 2002 (*Bonnichsen III*) and the Ninth Circuit Court of Appeals in 2004 (*Bonnichsen IV*).

American Indian studies scholar Kimberly TallBear has written extensively about relationships among race, genetics, and indigeneity (2001, 2003, 2007). For instance, she has critically engaged the emergence of DNA testing technologies as measurements of "true" Indianness and discusses "how the view of race as a fixed and natural division among people is perpetuated in the racialization of American Indian tribes and American Indian or Native American . . . ethnicity more broadly" (2003:82).[29] TallBear locates what seem to be novel contemporary struggles over identity in a historical perspective that emphasizes the centrality of colonization. I use some of her insights here to suggest that legal reckoning of Kennewick Man as *not* Native American under NAGPRA is part of this burgeoning landscape of *genetic indigeneity*, a landscape wherein claims to and conflicts over "Who is Indian?" are racialized and geneticized. Further, I suggest that the scientific and legal categorization of Kennewick Man as somehow *pre*-indigenous emerges at a time wherein investigations of potential relationships between race and genes are being reformulated as central questions both in the genomic sciences and in the public sphere more generally, especially in the United States. From large-scale human genetic variation projects (Hamilton 2008a) to genetic ancestry tracing technologies (Bolnick et al. 2007; TallBear 2003) to agendas in biomedical research (Rose 2007), the power of what anthropologist Duana Fullwiley calls "the molecularization of race" has thus far been expansive in its reach in the science of the twenty-first century (2007a; see also Fullwiley 2007b; Wald 2006).

In her discussion of the role of genetic identification in rendering indigenous peoples legally "visible" to settler courts, legal scholar Karen O'Connell argues that "[i]ndigenous peoples are forced to present themselves before law and science as invisible peoples requesting embodiment, as possessing no set identity and requiring a legal determination of their status"

(2007:38). O'Connell's observation that "the promise of genetic technologies is at the same time a continuation of their attempts to deny or obliterate indigenous presence" is especially revealing (2007:38). The defendants' efforts to embody the Ancient One as indigenous ancestor, as Native American under the NAGPRA statute, is countered by the plaintiffs' attempts to embody Kennewick Man as "Caucasoid," as "Paleo-American," and thus as *pre*-indigenous (see also Watkins 2004). In the *Bonnichsen* court, the competing attempts to legally embody Kennewick Man demonstrate some of the stakes in this contemporary reckoning of "Who is Indian?"

It is important to remember that although researchers were able to extract DNA samples from the remains, none of these samples could withstand the rigors of testing, and scientists were unable to make any determinations about Kennewick Man's "genes." Thus, legal and scientific allusions to the "genetic" in this case are literally without referent.[30] Such allusions nevertheless mirror the problematic assumption that phenotype, expressed in this case in the language of morphology, and genotype are closely linked in visually apparent ways. These allusions further reflect the presumption that morphological difference—especially in its racial idiom—points to more fundamental group differences at the level of the genome and that earlier scientific modes of constituting human groups have been straightforwardly "confirmed" by genetic science.[31] These presumptions were crucial in providing an interpretive foundation for the argument that Kennewick Man was not Native American under NAGPRA.

KENNEWICK MAN: "NATIVE" OR "AMERICAN"?

> The chronological information needed to make the determination that the Kennewick skeletal remains are "Native American" as defined by NAGPRA has been provided by the additional C14 testing conducted by the Department of the Interior and three radiocarbon laboratories. All the dates obtained predate 6000 BP and are clearly pre-Columbian [Letter from the Secretary of the Interior, September 21, 2000].

Contrary to the DOI's finding "that proper disposition of the Kennewick remains based upon cultural affiliation and aboriginal occupation is to the [tribal] claimants," the Ninth Circuit Court of Appeals ruled that NAGPRA "unambiguously requires that human remains bear some relationship to a *presently existing* tribe, people, or culture to be considered Native American" (*Bonnichsen IV*:5065; emphasis in original).

> Human remains that are 8340 to 9200 years old and that bear only incidental genetic resemblance to modern-day American Indians, along with incidental genetic resemblance to other peoples, cannot be said to be the Indians' "ancestors" within Congress's meaning.

Congress enacted NAGPRA to give American Indians control over the remains of their genetic and cultural forbearers, not over the remains of people bearing no special and significant genetic or cultural relationship to some presently existing indigenous tribe, people, or culture [*Bonnichsen IV*:5072].

The *Bonnichsen* court's claim that "the record does not permit the Secretary [of the Interior] to conclude reasonably that Kennewick Man shares special and significant genetic or cultural features with presently existing indigenous tribes" challenges some of the fundamental premises upon which claims to indigeneity are based. Inhering in the term itself is reference to central temporal dimensions of indigeneity—most notably the idea that indigenous peoples are the descendants of human groups that preceded the settlement of the Americas by Europeans. Legal scholar Sarah Harding notes an irony in *Bonnichsen*, especially in terms of litigating indigenous rights in (post)colonial courts:

The marker on the timeline dividing pre-and post-European settlement has been used to effectively terminate most Native claims. Aboriginal identity has been defined by the courts as a historical artifact, something that existed in the past, in the time before European contact. Aboriginal peoples could take some solace in the fact that whereas the strength of their claims are perceived to have weakened with the passage of time, claims clearly traceable to precolonial times were more likely to succeed—a presumption built into NAGPRA. *Bonnichsen* undermines this one temporal advantage. The precolonial period on the timeline is no longer presumed to be the exclusive domain of Native American culture, despite the absence of any persuasive alternative story about the existence of other unrelated cultures (2005:260).

Thus, what Harding calls the "one temporal advantage" of indigeneity is rendered ineffectual by the *Bonnichsen* court through appeal to "the absence of evidence that Kennewick Man and modern tribes share significant genetic or cultural features" (see also Ripley 2005; Tsosie 1999).

The age of Kennewick Man's remains, given the limited studies to date, makes it almost impossible to establish any relationship between the remains and presently existing American Indians. At least no significant relationship has yet been shown. We cannot give credence to an interpretation of NAGPRA advanced by the government and the Tribal Claimants that would apply its provisions to remains that have at most a tenuous, unknown, and unproven connection, asserted solely because of the geographical location of the find (*Bonnichsen IV*:5072).

Dussias argues that the *Bonnichsen* court's reasoning here in effect creates a third category: "individuals who are descendants of pre-contact inhabitants of the United States but whom the court will not consider 'Native American'" (2005:134). This line of reasoning marks a key point of rhetorical departure in the Kennewick Man case wherein a primary scientific determinant of indigeneity shifts from age to genetics.

Following the plaintiffs' arguments, District Court Justice John Jelderks challenged the defendants' position that the age of the remains themselves automatically renders them "Native American" under NAGPRA.

> Under the Defendants' interpretation, possibly long-extinct immigrant peoples who may have differed significantly—genetically and culturally—from any surviving groups, would all be uniformly classified as "Native American" based solely on the age of their remains. All pre-Columbian people, no matter what group they belonged to, where they came from, how long they or their group survived, or how greatly they differed from the ancestors of present-day American Indians, would be arbitrarily classified as "Native American" and their remains and artifacts could be placed totally off-limits to scientific study (*Bonnichsen III*:29).

The appeals court characterized as "extreme" and "absurd" the suggestion "that the finding of any remains in the United States *in and of itself* would automatically render these remains 'Native American'" (*Bonnichsen IV*:5070; emphasis in original). Instead, the court shifts the focus to what it sees as a lack of connection between Kennewick Man and contemporary tribes and thus rules that Kennewick Man is not Native American under NAGPRA.

> The administrative record contains no evidence—let alone substantial evidence—that Kennewick Man's remains are connected by some special or significant genetic or cultural relationship to any presently existing indigenous tribe, people, or culture. An examination of the record demonstrates the absence of evidence that Kennewick Man and modern tribes share significant genetic or cultural features (*Bonnichsen IV*:5073).

But neither does the record *disprove* any genetic or cultural connection. Further, the language in NAGPRA reads that tribes "recognized as aboriginally occupying the area in which the objects were discovered" have a legitimate claim to Native American remains and objects.[32] Harding notes what she see as "the court's failure to understand (or at least to openly acknowledge) the case as being about two very different but equally ambiguous and culturally determined visions of the past" (2005:250).

How, though, does one of these "ambiguous and culturally determined visions of the past" become enshrined as scientific-legal fact while the other does not?

> This is a case about the ancient human remains of a man who hunted and lived, or at least journeyed, in the Columbia Plateau an estimated 8340 to 9200 years ago, a time predating all recorded history from any place in the world, a time before the oldest cities of our world had been founded, a time so ancient that the pristine and untouched land and the primitive cultures that may have lived on it are not deeply understood by even the most well-informed men and women of our age [*Bonnichsen IV*:5053].

In writing the opinion for the Ninth Circuit Court of Appeal, Justice Ronald M. Gould temporally locates the remains of Kennewick Man in "a time predating all recorded history," "a time so ancient" that understanding is largely beyond "even the most well-informed men and women of our age." That Kennewick Man is indeed ancient is not up for debate. What is up for debate, however, is how his ancientness matters in the legal classification and ultimate disposition of his remains. As I discussed in the previous section, remains traditionally classified as "pre-Columbian" were usually presumed to be indigenous because of their age and the location in which they were found. Yet in *Bonnichsen*, the plaintiff-scientists argue for, and the courts accept, a classificatory schema that asserts a kind of *pre*-indigenous classification (see Fish 2006; Harding 2005; Ripley 2005; Watkins 2004). Legal scholar S. Alan Ray argues that "the court's analysis rendered irrelevant how Native peoples construct their own lives and their own definitions of 'Native American,' and therefore render unintelligible how tribal claimants were able to recognize an ancestor in the Ancient One" (2006:94). I further suggest not only that indigenous epistemologies and ethical systems were rendered irrelevant to and unintelligible in the *Bonnichsen* court, but also that the deeply cultural nature of the epistemological and ethical claims of the plaintiff-scientists were made *invisible* under the rubric scientific fact. Thus, the court legally reinscribes pre-Columbian remains as "genetically and culturally" different from contemporary American Indian groups. Legal understandings of science work to ensure that Kennewick Man's indigeneity is effaced which in turn makes him available to the plaintiff-scientists for further study.

The historical and legal processes that create the modern category of Native American are occluded, and a particular legal standard of "Native American" is created and imposed to limit indigenous property claims and access to the Ancient One. Dussias notes a particular irony in the legal and scientific battle over Kennewick Man: "The spoils of past plundering of Native American remains did not provide as complete a sample as would have been required to draw conclusions in which more confidence could have been placed" (2005:139). Or, as TallBear argues:

What is crucial in the fight for meaning between indigenous peoples and scientists is the historically colonial nature of how science has arrived at its origin narratives. In their quest to understand human origins and migratory history in the "Americas," the evidence gathered by scientists has come from indigenous peoples' bodies and from the remains of ancestors that lie or should lie in their historic lands (2007:422).[33]

In 2005, National Geographic, in concert with IBM and the Waite Family Foundation, launched the *The Genographic Project* "to map humanity's genetic journey through the ages."[34] Again, despite the lack of genetic material, Kennewick Man is included in the virtual, interactive "Atlas of the Human Journey" on the Genographic Project's website, which claims, "By mapping the appearance and frequency of genetic markers in modern peoples, we create a picture of when and where ancient humans moved around the world." If the user visits the section of the atlas labeled 10,000–5000 BC, he or she will find a link to Kennewick Man. On the map, the point that marks the location of Kennewick Man's 1996 (re)discovery in modern-day Washington State is traversed by an imagined migratory path labeled by the letters C and D. When the user follows this path, he or she will learn that C and D represent genetic markers (mtDNA), each "one of five mitochondrial lineages found in aboriginal Americans." [35] Perhaps, then, this raises the question of whether or not, post-*Bonnichsen*, it is safe for Kennewick Man to be indigenous again.

CONCLUSION: ANCIENT DNA AND CONTEMPORARY INDIGENEITY

The biological reification of race occurs in two ways: what is cultural or social is represented as natural or biological, and what is dynamic, relative, and continuous is represented as static, absolute, and discrete [Gannett 2004:340].

Making the world, building narratives is a craft, and we need to become skilled at that craft. We must learn to notice the networks of systems that sustain geneticization and identify some of the conceptual barriers that have made these networks so difficult to trace [Lindee et al. 2003:17].

In 2005, following the ruling of the Appeals Court, the remains of Kennewick Man were turned over to be stored at the Burke Museum of Natural History and Culture at the University of Washington in Seattle.[36] Since that time, scientists have conducted a series of studies on the remains, and these studies have generated new findings in physical anthropology and related disciplines. The decision in *Bonnichsen v. United States* continues to be controversial and debates over the language of NAGPRA have entered a new era of legal wrangling.[37] Both because of financial constraints and concern that the US Supreme Court would uphold the appeals court ruling, the tribal coalition chose not pursue further action in *Bonnichsen*. Instead, NAGPRA proponents have generally focused on changing the language in the statute to better reflect the needs of tribes and to prevent rulings similar to *Bonnichsen* in the future.[38]

Bonnichsen is but one example of how new terrains of science such as genetics are being rearticulated in older terms, most notably in the familiar terms of "discovery." Peter Fitzpatrick reminds us that the Euro-American doctrine of discovery that undergirded colonization in the Americas is not simply "an antiquarian exercise" but rather a modern one "in the sense of having current significance, of discovery's still being an impelling force in the treatment of peoples supposedly once discovered and in the self-identity of those who would claim to have once discovered them . . ." (2000). Just as colonizers once laid claim to parts of the Americas under the rubric of *terra nullius*—uninhabited land—so the courts constructed Kennewick Man as a kind of *corpus nullius*, as "unknown and apparently unknowable" (*Bonnichsen III*:31).[39] Thus, in the *Bonnichsen* rulings, Kennewick Man is legally rediscovered as Paleo-American, as pre-indigenous, and as *not* Native American.

I have argued throughout this chapter that the rendering of indigeneity in genetic terms is a key rhetorical strategy deployed by the court, one with an important history and profound material consequences. *Bonnichsen* signals the need for continuing attention to the ways in which colonial "blood logics" (see Kauanui 2002) represent what Richard W. Perry calls "layered mappings of spatial difference inherited from earlier ethno-racial and colonial governmental forms" (2006:127). Further, in a time when maps and measurements of one's "genetic ancestry" are increasingly available to an interested public, we must pay particular attention to how these technologies are translated into, or how they overlay, new political and legal modes of classification (Hamilton 2008b).

My purpose here was to trace some of the processes through which genetic knowledge is produced and deployed, and to further examine how such knowledge production articulates with other sociopolitical, economic, and cultural processes (see also Faubion and Hamilton 2007). In closing, I suggest that genetic identity, and more specifically genetic indigeneity, is an emergent dimension in a larger political economy of recognition. The present discussion of the *Bonnichsen* litigation provides but one example of contemporary legal and scientific claims to the importance of relationships among genetics, race and identity.

Notes

NOTES TO CHAPTER 1

1. In this context, I use the term North American to refer only to indigenous peoples in Canada and the United States. Further, I use the term indigenous to refer to a heterogeneous group of people who are the descendants of populations who lived in North America prior to European contact and colonization.
2. For further conceptualization of indigeneity and its multiple dimensions, see e.g., Cadena and Starn 2007; Clifford 1988; 2001; Darian-Smith 2004; Landzelius 2006; Li 2000; Miller 2003; Richland 2007; Weaver 2000.
3. Some examples of legal histories of the American and Canadian Wests are Asher 1999; Baker 1999; Foster 1994, 1995; Harring 1994, 1998; Knafla 1986; Knafla and Swainger 2005; Loo 1994, 1995; McLaren et al. 1992.
4. See e.g., Cairns 1999; Gordon and Newfield 1996; Minow 1995; Okin et al. 1999; Povinelli 2002; Sarat and Kearns 1995, 1999.
5. Some, in fact, have expressed concern that those who urge us to move beyond the culture concept are part of a continuing colonialist model, one which short-circuits one of the most powerful discursive tools available to indigenous peoples and other oppressed groups (e.g., Maybury-Lewis 2002).
6. For some of these ongoing discussions in anthropology, see e.g., Barnard 2006; Kuper 2003; Lee 2006.
7. The insights of the Critical Race Theory movement have been invaluable to these kinds of critical engagements. See e.g., Aylward 1999; Crenshaw 1995; Delgado and Stefancic 1997, 2000, 2001.

NOTES TO CHAPTER 2

1. For a discussion of high incarceration rates among American Indians, see Greenfeld and Smith 1999. For a specific discussion of racism and its relationship to the criminalization of American Indians, see Ross 1998.
2. See e.g., D. Germain, *Chicago Sun-Times*, "Teens' Banishment by Tribal Court Seen as a Failure," September 10, 1995; M. Sangiacomo, *Plain Dealer*, "Judge Admits Teens' Banishment a Failure," August 30, 1995.
3. See, for instance, T.W. Haines, *The Seattle Times*, "Banishment Order Sparks Tribal Feud--Tlingit Faction's Authority Disputed," July 17, 1994.; I. Lobos, *The Seattle Times*, "Native Group Challenges Authority of Tlingit Judge," September 13, 1994.

4. For an excellent overview of the restorative justice literature, see Menkel-Meadow 2007. For critiques of restorative justice, see Acorn 2004; Daly 2002.
5. For a broader discussion of the institutionalization of "alternatives" to court in the United States, see Harrington 1985; Harrington and Merry 1988; Merry and Milner 1993.
6. For a critique of the colonial invention of tradition, see most famously Hobsbawm and Ranger 1983.
7. Thirty-one to forty-one months for Guthrie; fifty-one months for Roberts.
8. *Tacoma News Tribune*, "Judge agrees to tribe's exile law," July 7, 1994:B1.
9. *Tacoma News Tribune*, "Doubts raised over plan to exile teens," July 26, 1994:B6.
10. P. Andersen, *Tacoma News Tribune*, "Tlingit judgment put on hold," July 30, 1994:A6.
11. Ibid.:sidebar.
12. Ibid.:A6.
13. D. Glamser, *USA Today*, "Alaskan teens' prison may be the great outdoors," August 12–14, 1994:13A.
14. M. Campobasso, *Tacoma News Tribune*, "Judge lets pair face exile by tribal court/Tlingit youths may be banished to remote island for robbery," August 13, 1994:B6.
15. R. Meyerowitz, *Tacoma News Tribune*, "Tlingit judge's credibility questioned," August 28, 1994:B8.
16. *Tacoma News Tribune*, "Judge clears way for banishment/Allows tribe to punish teens who beat man," August 25, 1994:B8.
17. R. Meyerowitz, *Tacoma News Tribune*, "Tlingit judge's credibility questioned," August 28, 1994:B8.
18. Ibid.
19. Ibid.
20. B. Akre, *Tacoma News Tribune*, "Tlingit teens stand before elders to account for criminal assault," September 2, 1994:B6.
21. B. Akre, *Tacoma News Tribune*, "Solitary confinement without the walls," September 4, 1994:A8.
22. B. Akre, *Tacoma News Tribune*, "Tlingit teens stand before elders to account for criminal assault," September 2, 1994:B6.
23. Ibid.
24. B. Akre, *Tacoma News Tribune*, "Tlingit elders to banish 2 teen offenders to islands," September 3 1994:A1.
25. Ibid.
26. Ibid.
27. *Tacoma News Tribune*, "Tlingit 'council' can't do worse than state," September 10, 1994:A10.
28. B. Akre, *Tacoma News Tribune*, "Tlingit elders to banish 2 teen offenders to islands," September 3 1994:A1.
29. *Tacoma News Tribune*, "Tribal vote rejects court that banished 2 teens," September 30, 1994:B9.
30. *Tacoma News Tribune*, "Banishment said to be working," November 17, 1994:B6.
31. The youths' possession of shotguns became a point of contention later on when the prosecution argued it contravened Allendoerfer's ruling that no firearms be allowed. The Tlingit tribal court argued the boys needed shotguns to protect them in the wild.
32. *Tacoma News Tribune*, "Banishment said to be working," November 17, 1994:B6. It should also be noted, however, that Theodore Roberts, grandfa-

ther of Simon Roberts, was a tribal judge on the Kuye'di Kuiu Kwaan Tribal Court.

33. *Tacoma News Tribune*, "The area briefly--Snohomish County: prosecutor seeks return of banished teens," April 2, 1995:B2. The type of firearm the boys possessed is unclear.
34. Ibid.
35. Ibid.
36. *Tacoma News Tribune*, "Banished Tlingit teens still face prison, Washington appeals court rules," May 2, 1995:B4.
37. *Washington State v. Roberts, et al.* 77 Wn. App. 678, 894 P.2d 1340 (1995).
38. *New York Times Current Events Edition*, "2 Indians who accepted exile still face prison, court rules," May 2, 1995:A17.
39. *Tacoma News Tribune*, "Teens opt to finish exile before sentencing," July 8, 1995:B6.
40. *Tacoma News Tribune*, "Banished teen seen in town/Tribal court had sent 18-year-old to island," July 23, 1995:B3.
41. *Tacoma News Tribune*, "Visits interfere with progress of banished teens, expert finds," July 27,1995:B3.
42. *Tacoma News Tribune*, "Teens' banishment called a failure/Report says youths travel, get help from families," September 10, 1995:B9.
43. Ibid.
44. Ibid.:B4.
45. *Tacoma News Tribune*, "Banished Tlingit duo jailed," October 4, 1995:B1.
46. According to an *Associated Press* report, Guthrie has been arrested for drunken driving, assault, and disorderly conduct (P. Andersen, *Tacoma News Tribune*, "Tlingit judgment put on hold," July 30, 1994:A6). According to a *Seattle Times* report, he was arrested for attempting to buy alcohol as a minor, writing bad cheques, and ignored a request to talk to police (R. Denn, *Seattle Times*, "Tlingit man gets another chance," November 20, 1997).
47. Guthrie was supposed to make restitution payments to the court in the amount of $43,000. The money is earmarked for the state Department of Labor and Industries, which covered Whittlesey's medical bills and lost wages (*Seattle Times*, "Tlingit man who served banishment for assault ordered to pay restitution," August 13, 1997).
48. *Seattle Times*, "Tlingit man who served banishment for assault ordered to pay restitution," August 13, 1997.
49. Spivak would later express disappointment with the oversimplified ways in which the phrase "strategic essentialism" was used: "my notion just simply became the union ticket for essentialism....So, as a phrase, I have given up on it. As to whether I have given up on it as a project, that is really a different idea" Danius et al. 1993:35.
50. In her examination of nineteenth-century American Indian writings, Cheryl Walker rightly points out that many academic narratives about the encounters between settler populations and indigenous peoples have a tendency to characterize the effects of these encounters as unidirectional [1997].
51. See also James Riding In's account of the extension of US criminal jurisdiction over the Pawnee in Nebraska (2002).
52. *Ex Parte Crow Dog*, 109 US 556, 3 S.Ct. 396, 27 L.Ed. 1030 (1883).
53. *Major Crimes Act* (18 USC § 1153). For a more extensive discussion of the Major Crimes Act, see e.g., Harring 1994 and Olund 2002.
54. *Ex parte Tiger*, 47 SW 304 (1898).
55. Interview conducted by author, March 1998.

56. The Indian Reorganization Act (IRA) is also known as the Wheeler-Howard Act. For a further discussion of the development of American Indian self-governance in the United States, see Robbins 1992; Taylor 1980.
57. Allendoerfer used a legal mechanism known as *deferred sentencing.* It is usually used in cases wherein defendants are addicts and need to participate in a rehabilitation program prior to serving their prison sentences.
58. *Tacoma News Tribune*, "Give Tlingits a chance," July 18, 1994:A6.; see also, *Tacoma News Tribune*, "Tlingit 'council' can't do worse than state," September 10, 1994:A10.
59. C. Sileo, *Insight on the News*, "When Cultures Clash, Should Punishment Fit the Criminal?" October 24, 1994:9.

NOTES TO CHAPTER 3

1. *The Globe and Mail*, "Bishop may avoid trial," June 12, 1998:A9.
2. B. Daisley, *The Lawyer's Weekly*, "Sex Charge Resolved by Native Healing Circle," July 10, 1998.
3. ibid.
4. Further, O'Connor had already served six months in jail, almost as much time as he would need to serve in prison on the rape charge before becoming eligible for parole.
5. Comment attributed to assistant deputy attorney-general, Ernie Quantz. *Vancouver Sun*, "O'Connor appeal dropped after healing circle," June 18, 1998:A1.
6. B. McLintock, *The Province*, "Healing Circle Built on Respect and Equality," June 18, 1998.
7. Ibid.
8. *Vancouver Sun*, "O'Connor Appeal Dropped after Healing Circle," June 18, 1998.
9. B. McLintock, *The Province*, "Finally, He Confesses," June 18, 1998.
10. Ibid.
11. Author's fieldnotes, June 2000. See also, P. Barnsley, *Windspeaker*, "Prosecution avoided; Bishop Hubert O'Connor apologizes for sexual abuse of residential school woman," August 1, 1998:4; R. Matas, *The Globe and Mail*, "Group wants bishop to face rape charge," June 19, 1998:A17.
12. For more detail on these movements, see Chapter 2.
13. See e.g., VARJP n.d.; Warhaft et al. 1999. For an excellent analysis of some of the tensions surrounding such projects, see Miller 2001.
14. For an extensive bibliography on Aboriginal women and the law, see Fiske et al. 1996.
15. These critiques challenge the offender-based/male-focused nature of restorative justice measures, asserting that, despite its claims to the contrary, victims are not integral to the process, and restorative justice projects generally work to decriminalize violence against women and children. Further, they contend that the position of indigenous women is already compromised by the patriarchal nature both of indigenous communities and mainstream societies and by the racist structure of Canadian society. Thus, restorative justice must be seen not only as "tradition" but also as an extension of institutionalized power.
16. This discourse of cultural sensitivity also undermines any explicit discussion of race and of how racism structures Canadian society, undercutting any analysis of indigenous peoples generally, and indigenous women in particular,

as a racialized group. See e.g., Dua and Robertson 1999; Razack 1998, 2002.

17. B. McLintock, *The Province*, "Healing Circle Built on Respect and Equality," June 18, 1998.
18. B. Daisley, *The Lawyer's Weekly*, "Sex Charge Resolved by Native Healing Circle," July 10, 1998.
19. *Vancouver Sun*, "O'Connor Appeal Dropped after Healing Circle," June 18, 1998.
20. Ibid.
21. See also Nader 1990, 2002.
22. *Vancouver Sun*, "O'Connor Appeal Dropped after Healing Circle," June 18, 1998.
23. For further discussion of some Catholic responses to the residential school issue, see Furniss 2000.
24. See e.g., Matoesian 1993.
25. A contention legally reinforced by the Canadian Supreme Court's 1997 decision that most of the land base in BC was never ceded. See *Delgamuukw v. British Columbia*, [1997] 3 S.C.R. 1010.
26. The Canadian Indian residential school system was in place from 1879 until 1986 (Milloy 1999).
27. As quoted in M. Montgomery, "The Six Nations and the MacDonald Franchise," *Ontario History* 57 (March 1965:13). Cited in Milloy 1999:6.
28. N.A.C. RG 10, Vol. 6039, File 160–1, MR C 8152, the Archbishop of St. Boniface to Honourable Sir [R. Rogers], November [?] 1912. Cited in Milloy 1999:27.
29. See e.g., Adams 1995; Furniss 2000; Milloy 1999. For first person accounts from survivors of the residential school system in British Columbia, see Jack 2006.
30. See e.g., Chrisjohn et al. 2002; for an intersectional analysis of the impact of juvenile detention centers on First Nations girls, see Sangster 2002.
31. For analyses of Goffman's concept as applied specifically to Indian residential schools, see Adams 1995 and Chrisjohn et al. 2002.
32. See e.g., Maurer and Merry 1997; Povinelli 2002b
33. Milloy also discusses the impact of abuse of the sexuality of indigenous children.
34. Bishop O'Connor died of a heart attack on July 24, 2007 at the age of 79.

NOTES TO CHAPTER 4

1. K. Makin and R. Mata, *The Globe and Mail*, "Reserve land worth half of market value," November 10, 2000:A3.
2. For a more in-depth discussion of the concept of landscape as well as the relationship among law, space and power, see e.g., Blomley, Delaney, and Ford 2001; Braun 1997; Hirsch and O'Hanlon 1995; Razack 2002b.
3. During 1999, Canadian news coverage of the Musqueam Park dispute was extensive; in Vancouver, the story was covered on an almost daily basis and rhetoric was often inflammatory and deeply racialized. See e.g., D. Rinehart, *Vancouver Sun*, "Feuds over Native lands flaring up across B.C.," January 16, 1999:A1; M. Jimenez, *National Post*, "BC residents balk at Native band's huge hike in leases," January 11, 1999.
4. See also Culhane 1998; Lambertson 1995; Mawani 2002; Razack 2002b; Roy 1989; Ward 1990.

5. For more information about the history of the Musqueam, see the Band's website: www.musqueam.bc.ca. See also Harris 2002; Muckle 1998; Weightman 1972.
6. See e.g., Blomley 1997; Mawani 2003.
7. This rhetoric was used widely by the leaseholders both in government protests and in media interviews.
8. As Said (1978) and others have pointed out, radically Other usually means inferior and this presumed inferiority is necessary for the constitution of the dominant identity. See Francis 1992 for a discussion of the importance of images of "Indian" in the Canadian culture.
9. E. Campbell, *Vancouver Sun*, "The land and the law: A chief states his people's case on Musqueam land rents, which he says is unrelated to other aboriginal issues," March 13, 1999:A21.
10. "In 1995 a 30-year fixed rate for the lease expired, and the band council demanded rent increases to match rents on homes just outside Musqueam property lines. The concept seemed reasonable, since homeowners had leased the land for several hundred dollars a year . . . but the rent increases amounted to 7000% or more. They sparked sticker shock and anger" (Frank 2000:20).
11. *BC Report*, July 26, 1999:26–27.
12. L. Culbert, "Musqueam residents go to Victoria to demand help with lease increases," *Vancouver Sun*, January 19, 1999:B4.
13. M. Hanvelt, *Vancouver Sun*, "Musqueam leases are a matter of law," October 1, 1999:A22.
14. For a discussion of the importance of First Nations labor in BC's capitalist expansion, see Knight 1996.
15. For analyses of settler Canadians' self-understandings as non-violent, non-racist and benevolent, see e.g., Bannerji 1996; Francis 1992; Mackey 1999; Razack 1998b, 1999, 2000.
16. T. Lautens, *Vancouver Sun*, "Musqueam lease debacle revs up bid to pass treaty," January 9, 1999:A23.
17. For discussions of legal constructions of whiteness, see e.g., Gross 1998; López 1996.
18. *National Post*, January 11, 1999:A6.
19. *National Post*, June 30, 1999:A19.
20. ibid.
21. *National Post*, "Ottawa to enforce rent ruling on Musqueam leaseholders," September 23, 1999:A11.
22. D. Rinehart, *Vancouver Sun*, "Feuds over Native lands flaring up across B.C.," January 16, 1999:A1.
23. *BC Business Magazine*, September 1996:36.
24. Dominy 1995.
25. See e.g., Cassidy 1992; Culhane 1998; Nadasdy 2002; Povinelli 2002a, 2004; Samson 2001; Seed 2001.
26. See Blomley 1996 for a discussion of First Nations activism in BC.
27. In the decade between 1986 and 1996, the number of non-indigenous residents living on Indian reserves in the province nearly doubled (Kesselman 2000).

NOTES TO CHAPTER 5

1. Native American Graves Protection and Repatriation Act, 25 USC 3001 et seq. [Nov. 16, 1990].

2. The five Northwest tribes were the Umatilla, the Yakama, the Nez Perce, the Wanapum, and the Colville. Throughout the chapter, I refer to the Ancient One—Kennewick Man only as Kennewick Man for ease of use and because that is largely how the courts and the media refer to him.

3. In addition to the scientists, a fringe religious group called the Asatru Folk Assembly also claimed Kennewick Man based on his "Caucasoid" nature. I do not concentrate on their claims here because they were not central to the legal process. In 2000, the Asatru Folk Assembly gave up their legal battle. See e.g., M. Lee, *Tri-City Herald*, "Asatru to give up Kennewick battle," January 14, 2000. See also, Downey 2000 and Thomas 2000 for more information.

4. For a discussion of the early days of the dispute, see Thomas 2000.

5. T. Egan, *The New York Times*, "Old skull gets white looks, stirring dispute," April 2, 1998:A12; B. Dietrich, *The Seattle Times*, "Ancient Bones, Ancient Disputes—Is Kennewick Skeleton 'Asian' or 'European'?" August 29, 1996: A1.

6. *Bonnichsen v. United States*, 969 F.Supp. 614 [hereafter *Bonnichsen I*].

7. *Bonnichsen v. United States*, 367 E 3d 864 (9th Cir. 2004) [hereafter *Bonnichsen IV*]; *Bonnichsen v. United States*, 217 F.Supp.2d 1116 (D.Or.2002) [*Bonnichsen III*]; *Bonnichsen v. United States*, 969 F.Supp. 628 (D.Or.1997) [*Bonnichsen II*].

8. See e.g., Afrasiabi 1997; Downey 2000; Dussias 2005; Flood 2002; Harding 2005; Slayman 1997; Thomas 2000; Tsosie 1999, 2005; Watkins 2004; Zimmerman 2005.

9. For a discussion of the American Indian repatriation movement and the development of NAFTA, see Echo-Hawk and Echo-Hawk 1994; Fine-Dare 2002; Mihesuah 2000; Trope and Echohawk 1998. For cultural and ethical perspectives on the reburial of ancestors, see e.g., Harper 2001; Yellow Bird and Milun 1994.

10. And, as Rebecca Tsosie notes, the passage of NAGPRA itself also facilitated further research on remains in museum and university collections (1999:624). See also Rose et al. 1996.

11. For a more general history of biological anthropology, see Stocking 1988.

12. For discussions of some of the specific uses of racial science in Indian country, see e.g., Beaulieu 1984; Deloria Jr. 1997; Riding In 1992.

13. See e.g., Baker 1998; Bieder 1986, 2000; Gould 1996; Graves 2001; Haller 1971; Smedley 1999; Stepan 1982. For a specific discussion of racial science and its implications for Indian policy, see Prucha 1982.

14. As Roger Echo-Hawk and Larry Zimmerman argue, racialism has been a key part of American archaeology, despite persistent disavowals of the "biological reality of race" (2006).

15. In my analysis here, I refer specifically to the modes of inquiry and disciplinary commitments of the scientist-plaintiffs and their supporters because they are the purveyors of the "scientific" to the *Bonnichsen* court. Readers should appreciate that there are many different viewpoints among physical anthropologists and archaeologists concerning the disposition of human remains as well as the role and content of scientific study. As Devon Mihesuah aptly states, "Within the anthropological profession there are radically different opinions about repatriation, the role and responsibilities of archaeologists, and the definition of 'ethics'" (2000:8). See e.g., Fforde *et al.* 2002; Jones and Stapp 2003; Kerber 2006; Mihesuah 2000; Trigger 2003; Turner 2005; Watkins 2000, 2005.

16. For an extensive discussion of the term "Caucasian," see Baum 2007.

17. See e.g., Downey 2000; Johansen 2004; Preston 1997; Thomas 2000. For a more extensive discussion of media portrayals of the controversy, see Coleman and Dysart 2005.
18. Sculptor Tom McClelland has published a brochure entitled, "The Facial Reconstruction of Kennewick Man," which briefly outlines the process he and Chatters used to create the mold. http://www.triartgallery.com/download/KennewickManBrochure.pdf (accessed April 27, 2008). McClelland also has a website with a more detailed account:http://www.tom-mcclelland.com/kennewickMan.htm (accessed April 27, 2008).
19. A photograph of the model first appeared in Douglas Preston's *New Yorker* article, "The Face of Kennewick Man," (1998:53). A 3-D QuickTime version of the Chatters' and McClelland's model is available on *Nova*'s companion website to its documentary, *Mystery of the First Americans*, first aired in February 2000:http://www.pbs.org/wgbh/nova/first/kennewickvr.html (accessed April 26, 2008). The image also graces the cover of Chatters' book, *Ancient Encounters* (2001).
20. E.g., Downey 2000:134–135. Images linking the original Kennewick Man model and Stewart have been extensively reproduced (and critiqued), and, at the time of writing in 2008, were still widely available on the internet.
21. Chatters himself repeats this metaphor in *Ancient Encounters* (2001:146).
22. For some specific discussions of scientific representation in the area of paleoanthropology, see Berman 1999; Milun 2001; Sommer 2006, 2007.
23. Readers can access this image at the Time Magazine online archive, http://www.time.com/time/covers/0,16641,20060313,00.html (accessed April 26, 2008).
24. A. King, *Tri-City Herald*, "Kennewick Man graces Time Cover," March 7, 2006; http://www.tri-cityherald.com/1211/story/136626.html (accessed April 26, 2008).
25. Chatters 1997. Reproduced at http://www.mnh.si.edu/arctic/html/kennewick_man.html (accessed May 1, 2008). No such qualification was included in Preston's *New Yorker* story.
26. Difficult, although not impossible. American Indian scholar and activist Vine Deloria, Jr. has argued that the Chatters/McClelland model bears a striking resemblance to Sauk Chief Black Hawk from an 1833 portrait (Thomas 2000:xxiii). Anthropologist Jonathan Marks has suggested that Kennewick Man looks as much like basketball great Patrick Ewing as he does Patrick Stewart (2002:235). See also the 3-D computer-aided forensic facial reconstruction of Kennewick Man in a *National Geographic* story, "Hunt for the First Americans" (Parfit and Garrett 2000) constructed from Chatters' original model of Kennewick Man's skull. This latter reconstruction looks very different from the Picard model.
27. This contention is not without critics. For instance, *Harper's Magazine* writer Jack Hitt discusses Chatters' longstanding equivocations around terms such as Caucasoid, Caucasian, European, and white (2005:51).
28. This image is reproduced at http://www.triartgallery.com/index.php?ID=28 (accessed May 5, 2008).
29. See also Beckenhauer 2003; de Plevitz and Croft 2003; Johnston 2003; O'Connell 2007; Parry and Elliott 2002.
30. "No DNA suitable for PCR amplification could be extracted from the Kennewick samples studied. Thus, no conclusion regarding its ethnic ancestry or cultural affiliation based on DNA can be made" (Smith et al. 2000). Reports from other studies conducted on the remains can be found at the National Park Service's Kennewick Man website:http://www.nps.gov/archeology/kennewick/index.htm.

31. There is an extensive critical literature challenging some of these presumptions especially as they concern the relationship between genetics and race (e.g., Bolnick et al. 2007; Duster 2003; El-Haj 2007; Fullwiley 2007b; Marks 2002; Smedley and Smedley 2005; Smedley 2006). See also the Social Sciences Research Council web forum, "Is Race 'Real'?" http://raceandgenomics.ssrc.org/.

32. 25 USC 3002, sec. 3.

33. Like anthropology, population genetics has also relied on conceptions of indigenous difference to develop as a discipline. Reardon points to the centrality of indigenous peoples—and indigenous peoples' genetic materials—in the development of the HGDP and outlines how conceptions of indigeneity were paramount to how genetic variation research was both imagined and implemented (2005; see also Lock 1999; Santos 2003). Indigenous critics have pointed to the similarities between earlier scientific practices such as craniology and what they term biocolonialism (e.g., Guerrero 2003; Harry et al. 2000; Harry 2002; see also Marks 2005; Whitt 1998).

34. https://www3.nationalgeographic.com/genographic/about.html (accessed May 18, 2008).

35. https://www3.nationalgeographic.com/genographic/atlas.html (accessed May 11, 2008). TallBear, among others, has importantly noted that "none of these markers is exclusive to Native American populations—all can be found in other populations around the world. They simply occur with more frequency in Native American populations" (2003:84).

36. See http://www.washington.edu/burkemuseum/kman/ (accessed March 17, 2008).

37. See e.g., A. Cary, *Tri-City Herald*, "Hastings says rule change would hurt science," Jan 18, 2008, http://www.tri-cityherald.com/1211/story/57914.html (accessed May 16, 2008). For news updates on the Kennewick Man story, see the "Kennewick Man Virtual Interpretive Center" sponsored by the *Tri-City Herald* at http://www.tri-cityherald.com/kman.

38. For updates on NAGPRA, see the National Park Service's "National NAGPRA" website, http://www.nps.gov/nagpra.

39. Anthropologist Patrick Wolfe recently used the term *corpus nullius* "to express the outer limit of othering that is reached when, as in the case of nineteenth-century US Indian policy, particular humans are excepted from the general requirements that govern the treatment of humanity as a whole" (2007:127). I am using it here in a more modest sense to suggest that that legal discourse works to render Kennewick Man as an "empty body," as a body that belongs to no one, that can then be "discovered" by the scientist-plaintiffs.

Bibliography

Aboriginal Women's Action Network
2001   The Implications of Restorative Justice for Aboriginal Women and Children Survivors of Violence: A Comparative Overview of Five Communities in British Columbia. Vancouver: Aboriginal Women's Action Network.

Acorn, Annalise E.
2004   Compulsory Compassion: A Critique of Restorative Justice. Vancouver: University of British Columbia Press.

Adams, David Wallace
1995   Education for Extinction: American Indians and the Boarding School Experience, 1875–1928. Lawrence: University Press of Kansas.

Afrasiabi, Peter R.
1997   Property Rights in Ancient Human Skeletal Remains. Southern California Law Review 70(3):36.

Amiotte, George
1996   The Eagle and the Raven: Purification by Banishment. USA: Heaven Fire Productions and Vision Maker Video.

Armstrong, Derek
2000   Purchaser Discounting Behaviour in Musqueam and Salish Park, 1980–98. Pp. 1–21. Unpublished manuscript on file with author.

Asher, Brad
1999   Beyond the Reservation: Indians, Settlers, and the Law in Washington Territory, 1853–1889. Norman: University of Oklahoma Press.

Aylward, Carol A.
1999   Canadian Critical Race Theory: Racism and the Law. Halifax: Fernwood Publishing.

Backhouse, Constance
1999   Colour-Coded: A Legal History of Racism in Canada, 1900–1950. Toronto and Buffalo: University of Toronto Press.

Baker, H. Robert
1999   Creating Order in the Wilderness: Transplanting the English Law to Rupert's Land, 1835–51. Law and History Review 17(2).

Baker, Lee D.
1998   From Savage to Negro: Anthropology and the Construction of Race, 1896
          -1954. Berkeley: University of California Press.

Balfour, Gillian
2008   Falling between the Cracks of Retributive and Restorative Justice: The
          Victimization and Punishment of Aboriginal Women. Feminist Criminol-
          ogy 3(2):101–120.

Bannerji, Himani
1996   On the Dark Side of the Nation: Politics of Multiculturalism and the State
          of Canada. Journal of Canadian Studies 31(3):103–128.

Barman, Jean
1997/98 Taming Aboriginal Sexuality: Gender, Power, and Race in British Colum-
          bia, 1850–1900. BC Studies 115/116:237–266.

Barnard, Alan
2006   Kalahari Revisionism, Vienna and the "Indigenous Peoples" Debate.
          Social Anthropology 14(1):1–16.

Bateman, Rebecca
1997   Comparative Thoughts on the Politics of Aboriginal Assimilation. BC
          Studies 114:59–83.

Baum, Bruce D.
2006   The Rise and Fall of the Caucasian Race: A Political History of Racial
          Identity. New York: New York University Press.

Beaulieu, David L.
1984   Curly Hair and Big Feet: Physical Anthropology and the Implementation
          of Land Allotment on the White Earth Chippewa Reservation. American
          Indian Quarterly 8(4):281–314.

Beckenhauer, Eric
2003   Redefining Race: Can Genetic Testing Provide Biological Proof of Indian
          Ethnicity? Stanford Law Review 56(1):161–190.

Behrendt, Larissa
2000   Consent in a (Neo) Colonial Society: Aboriginal Women as Sexual and
          Legal 'Other'. Australian Feminist Studies 15(33):353–367.

Bellerose, Elizabeth
1993   Sentencing and Sexual Assault: Eurocentric and Aboriginal Approaches.
          Ottawa: National Association of Women and the Law.

Berman, Judith C.
1999   Bad Hair Days in the Paleolithic: Modern (Re)Constructions of the Cave
          Man. American Anthropologist 101(2):288–304.

Bieder, Robert E.
1986   Science Encounters the Indian, 1820–1880: The Early Years of American
          Ethnology. Norman: University of Oklahoma Press.

1998   A Brief Historical Survey of the Expropriation of American Indian Remains. *In* Readings in American Indian Law: Recalling the Rhythm of Survival. J. Carrillo, ed. Pp. 164–171. Philadelphia: Temple University Press.
2000   The Representations of Indian Bodies in Nineteenth-Century American Anthropology. *In* Repatriation Reader: Who Owns American Indian Remains? D. A. Mihesuah, ed. Pp. 19–36. Lincoln: University of Nebraska Press.

Biolsi, Thomas
2001   Deadliest Enemies: Law and the Making of Race Relations on and Off Rosebud Reservation. Berkeley: University of California Press.

Blomley, Nicholas
1996   "Shut the Province Down": First Nations Blockades in British Columbia, 1984–1995. BC Studies 111:5–35.
1997   Property, Pluralism and the Gentrification Frontier. Canadian Journal of Law and Society 12(2):187–218.
1998   Landscapes of Property. Law & Society Review 32(3):567–612.

Blomley, Nicholas K., David Delaney, and Richard T. Ford
2001   The Legal Geographies Reader: Law, Power, and Space. Oxford, UK and Malden, MA: Blackwell Publishers.

Bohannan, Paul
1957   Justice and Judgment among the Tiv. London and New York: Oxford University Press.

Bolnick, Deborah A., et al.
2007   The Science and Business of Genetic Ancestry Testing. Science 318(5849):399–400.

Bradford, William C.
2000   Reclaiming Indigenous Legal Autonomy on the Path to Peaceful Coexistence: The Theory, Practice and Limitations of Tribal Peacemaking in Indian Dispute Resolution. North Dakota Law Review 76:551–604.

Braithwaite, John
2002   Restorative Justice & Responsive Regulation. Oxford and New York: Oxford University Press.

Braun, Bruce
1997   Buried Epistemologies: The Politics of Nature in (Post)Colonial British Columbia. Annals of the Association of American Geographers 87(1):3–31.

Bridgeman, Jo, and Susan Millns
1998   Feminist Perspectives on Law: Law's Engagement with the Female Body. London: Sweet & Maxwell.

Brightman, Robert
1995   Forget Culture: Replacement, Transcendence, Relexification. Cultural Anthropology 10(4):509–546.

Brownell, Margo
2001   Who Is an Indian? Searching for an Answer to the Question at the Core of Federal Indian Law. University of Michigan Journal of Law Reform 34:275.

Cairns, Alan C.
1999   Citizenship, Diversity, and Pluralism: Canadian and Comparative Perspectives. Montreal: McGill-Queen's University Press.

Cameron, Angela
2006   Stopping the Violence: Canadian Feminist Debates on Restorative Justice and Intimate Violence. Theoretical Criminology 10(1):49–66.

Canby, William C., Jr.
1998   American Indian Law in a Nutshell. St. Paul, MN: West Group.

Carbonatto, Helene
1995   Expanding Intervention Options for Spousal Abuse: The Use of Restorative Justice. Wellington: Institute of Criminology.

Carrillo, Jo
1998   Readings in American Indian Law: Recalling the Rhythm of Survival. Philadelphia: Temple University Press.
2002   Getting to Survivance: An Essay about the Role of Mythologies in Law. PoLAR: Political and Legal Anthropology Review 25(1):37–47.

Cassidy, Frank
1992   Aboriginal Title in British Columbia: *Delgamuukw Vs. The Queen*. Winnipeg: Oolichan and the Institute for Research on Public Policy.

Chanock, Martin
1985   Law, Custom, and Social Order: The Colonial Experience in Malawi and Zambia. Cambridge and New York: Cambridge University Press.

Chatters, James C.
1997   Encounter with an Ancestor. Anthropology Newsletter 38(1):9–10.
2000   The Recovery and First Analysis of an Early Holocene Human Skeleton from Kennewick, Washington. American Antiquity 65(2):291–316.
2001   Ancient Encounters: Kennewick Man and the First Americans. New York: Simon & Schuster.

Chrisjohn, Roland David, Michael Maraun, and Sherri Lynn Young
2002   The Circle Game: Shadows and Substance in the Indian Residential School Experience in Canada. Penticton, BC: Theytus Books.

Churchill, Ward, and Glen T. Morris
1992   Key Indian Laws and Cases. *In* The State of Native America: Genocide, Colonization, and Resistance. M. A. Jaimes, ed. Pp. 13–22. Boston: South End Press.

Clifford, James
1988   The Predicament of Culture: Twentieth-Century Ethnography, Literature, and Art. Cambridge, MA: Harvard University Press.
2001   Indigenous Articulations. Contemporary Pacific 13(2):468–490.

Cohn, Bernard S.
1989   Law and the Colonial State in India. *In* History and Power in the Study
        of Law. J. Starr and J. F. Collier, eds. Pp. 131–152. Ithaca, NY: Cornell
        University Press.

Coker, Donna
2006   Restorative Justice, Navajo Peacemaking and Domestic Violence. Theo-
        retical Criminology 10(1):67–85.

Coleman, Cynthia-Lou, and Erin Dysart
2005   Framing of Kennewick Man against the Backdrop of a Scientific and Cul-
        tural Controversy. Science Communication 27(1):3–26.

Collier, Jane F.
1999   Models of Indigenous Justice in Chiapas, Mexico: A Comparison of State
        and Zina-Cauteco Visions. PoLAR: Political and Legal Anthropology
        Review 22(1):94–100.

Comaroff, Jean, and John L. Comaroff
1991   Of Revelation and Revolution. Chicago: University of Chicago Press.

Comaroff, John L.
1995   Ethnicity, Nationalism, and the Politics of Difference in an Age of Revolu-
        tion. *In* Perspectives on Nationalism and War. J. L. Comaroff and P. C.
        Stern, eds. Sydney: Gordon and Breach.

Comaroff, John L., and Simon Roberts
1981   Rules and Processes: The Cultural Logic of Disputes in an African Con-
        text. Chicago: University of Chicago Press.

Consedine, Jim
1999   Restorative Justice: Healing the Effects of Crime. Lyttelton, NZ: Plough-
        shares Publications.

Cove, John J.
1999   Cultural Relativism in the Americanist Tradition: From Anthropologi-
        cal Method to Indigenous Emancipation. *In* Theorizing the Americanist
        Tradition. R. Darnell and L. P. Valentine, eds. Pp. 108–120. Toronto:
        University of Toronto Press.

Cowlishaw, Gillian K.
2000   Censoring Race in 'Post-Colonial' Anthropology. Critique of Anthropol-
        ogy 20(2):23.

Cragg, Wesley
1992   The Practice of Punishment: Towards a Theory of Restorative Justice.
        London and New York: Routledge.

Crawford, Suzanne J.
2000   (Re)Constructing Bodies: Semiotic Sovereignty and the Debate over
        Kennewick Man. *In* Repatriation Reader: Who Owns American Indian
        Remains? D. A. Mihesuah, ed. Pp. 211–236. Lincoln: University of
        Nebraska Press.

Crenshaw, Kimberle
1995   Critical Race Theory: The Key Writings That Formed the Movement. New York: W.W. Norton & Co.

Culhane, Dara
1998   The Pleasure of the Crown: Anthropology, Law and First Nations. Burnaby, BC: Talonbooks.

Crnkovich, Mary
1995   The Role of the Victim in the Criminal Justice System--Circle Sentencing in Inuit Communities. Canadian Institute for the Administration of Justice Conference, Banff, AB, Pp. 1–33.
1996   A Sentencing Circle. Journal of Legal Pluralism 36:159–181.

Cunneen, Chris
1998   Community Conferencing and the Fiction of Indigenous Control. The Australian and New Zealand Journal of Criminology 30(3):292–311.

Daly, Kathleen
2002   Restorative Justice: The Real Story. Punishment & Society 4(1):55–79.

Danius, Sara, Stefan Jonsson, and Gayatri Chakravorty Spivak
1993   An Interview with Gayatri Chakravorty Spivak. boundary 2 20(2):24–50.

Darian-Smith, Eve
2004   New Capitalists: Law, Politics, and Identity Surrounding Casino Gaming on Native American Land. Belmont, CA: Wadsworth/Thomson Learning.

Darnell, Regna, and Lisa Philips Valentine
1999   Theorizing the Americanist Tradition. Toronto: University of Toronto Press.

de la Cadena, Marisol, and Orin Starn
2007   Indigenous Experience Today. Oxford and New York: Berg.

de Plevitz, Loretta, and Larry Croft
2003   Aboriginality under the Microscope: The Biological Descent Test in Australian Law. QUT Law & Justice Journal 3(1):1–17.

Deer, Sarah
2004   Toward an Indigenous Jurisprudence of Rape. Kansas Journal of Law and Public Policy 14:121–143.

Delgado, Richard, and Jean Stefancic
1997   Critical White Studies: Looking Behind the Mirror. Philadelphia: Temple University Press.
2000   Critical Race Theory: The Cutting Edge. Philadelphia: Temple University Press.
2001   Critical Race Theory: An Introduction. New York: New York University Press.

Deloria Jr., Vine
1997   Red Earth, White Lies: Native Americans and the Myth of Scientific Fact. Golden, CO: Fulcrum Publishers.

Denis, Claude
1997   We Are Not You: First Nations and Canadian Modernity. Peterborough, ON: Broadview Press.

Dickson-Gilmore, E. J., and Carol La Prairie
2005   Will the Circle Be Unbroken?: Aboriginal Communities, Restorative Justice, and the Challenges of Conflict and Change. Toronto and Buffalo: University of Toronto Press.

Dirlik, Arif
2001   Comment on Kirsch's Lost Worlds: Environmental Disaster, "Culture Loss," And the Law. Current Anthropology 42(2):182.

Dombrowski, Kirk
2002   The Praxis of Indigenism and Alaska Native Timber Politics. American Anthropologist 104(4):1062–1073.

Dominy, Michèle
1995   White Settler Assertions of Native Status. American Ethnologist 22(2):358–374.

Downey, Roger
2000   Riddle of the Bones: Politics, Science, Race, and the Story of Kennewick Man. New York: Copernicus.

Dumont, Clayton W.
2003   The Politics of Scientific Objections to Repatriation. Wicazo Sa Review 18(1):109–128.

Dunbar Residents' Association
n.d.   Pacific Spirit Regional Park. http://www.dunbar-vancouver.org/dra-recreation.htm (accessed August 2, 2005).

Dussias, Allison M.
2005   Kennewick Man, Kinship, and the "Dying Race": The Ninth Circuit's Assimilationist Assault on the Native American Graves Protection and Repatriation Act. Nebraska Law Review 84(1):55–161.

Duster, Troy
2003   Buried Alive: The Concept of Race in Science. In Genetic Nature/Culture: Anthropology and Science Beyond the Two-Culture Divide. A. H. Goodman, D. Heath, and M. S. Lindee, eds. Pp. 258–277. Berkeley: University of California Press.

Echo-Hawk, Roger C., and Walter R. Echo-Hawk
1994   Battlefields and Burial Grounds: The Indian Struggle to Protect Ancestral Graves in the United States. Minneapolis: Lerner Publications Co.

Echo-Hawk, Roger C., and Larry J. Zimmerman
2006   Beyond Racism: Some Opinions about Racialism and American Archaeology. American Indian Quarterly 30(3&4):461–485.

Ehrlich, Susan
2001   Representing Rape: Language and Sexual Consent. London and New York: Routledge.

El-Haj, Nadia Abu
2007   The Genetic Reinscription of Race. Annual Review of Anthropology
         36(1):283–300.

Faubion, James D., and Jennifer A. Hamilton
2007   Sumptuary Kinship. Anthropological Quarterly 80(3):553–559.

Fforde, Cressida, Jane Hubert, and Paul Turnbull
2002   The Dead and Their Possessions: Repatriation in Principle, Policy, and
         Practice. London and New York: Routledge.

Fine-Dare, Kathleen S.
2002   Grave Injustice: The American Indian Repatriation Movement and NAG-
         PRA. Lincoln: University of Nebraska Press.

Fish, Adam
2006   Indigenous Bodies in Colonial Courts: Anthropological Science and the
         (Physical) Laws of the Remaining Human. Wicazo Sa Review 21(1):77–
         95.

Fiske, Jo-Anne
1991   Colonization and the Decline of Women's Status: The Tsimshian Case.
         Feminist Studies 17(3):509–536.

Fiske, Jo-Anne, Patty Ginn, and Marie Paturel
1996   Aboriginal Women and the Law: An Annotated Bibliography. Prince
         George: Child Welfare Research Centre, University of Northern British
         Columbia.

Fitzpatrick, Peter
1999   Passions out of Place. *In* Laws of the Postcolonial. E. Darian-Smith and P.
         Fitzpatrick, eds. Pp. 39–59. Ann Arbor: University of Michigan Press.
2000   "Enacted in the Destiny of Sedentary Peoples": Racism, Discovery and
         the Grounds of Law. Murdoch University. http://wwwlaw.murdoch.edu.
         au/balayi/v1n1/fitzpatrick.shtml (accessed March 22, 2002).

Fleras, Augie
1996   The Politics of Jurisdiction: Indigenizing Aboriginal-State Relations. *In*
         Visions of the Heart: Canadian Aboriginal Issues. D. A. Long and O. P.
         Dickason, eds. Pp. 147–177. Toronto and Fort Worth: Harcourt Brace &
         Company Canada.

Flood, Maura
2002   "Kennewick Man" Or "Ancient One"?--a Matter of Interpretation. Mon-
         tana Law Review 63:39–90.

Foster, Hamar
1994   "the Queen's Law Is Better Than Yours": International Homicide in Early
         British Columbia. *In* Essays in the History of Canadian Law: Crime and
         Criminal Justice. Vol. V. J. Phillips, T. Loo, and S. Lewthwaite, eds. Pp.
         41–111. Toronto: University of Toronto Press.
1995   Essays in the History of Canadian Law: British Columbia and the Yukon.
         Toronto and Buffalo: University of Toronto Press.

Foucault, Michel
1995 Discipline and Punish: The Birth of the Prison. New York: Vintage Books.

Francis, Daniel
1992 The Imaginary Indian: The Image of the Indian in Canadian Culture. Vancouver: Arsenal Pulp Press.

Frank, Steven
2000 Getting Angry over Native Rights. Time Magazine (Canadian Edition) 155(20):16–24.

Frohmann, Lisa, and Elizabeth Mertz
1994 Legal Reform and Social Construction: Violence, Gender, and the Law. Law & Social Inquiry 19(4):829–851.

Fullwiley, Duana
2007a The Molecularization of Race: Institutionalizing Human Difference in Pharmacogenetics Practice. Science as Culture 16(1):1 - 30.
2007b Race and Genetics: Attempts to Define the Relationship. BioSocieties 2(2):221–237.

Furniss, Elizabeth
1997/98 Pioneers, Progress, and the Myth of the Frontier: The Landscape of Public History in Rural British Columbia. BC Studies 115/116:7–44.
1999 The Burden of History: Colonialism and the Frontier Myth in a Rural Canadian Community. Vancouver: University of British Columbia Press.
2000 Victims of Benevolence: The Dark Legacy of the Williams Lake Residential School. Vancouver: Arsenal Pulp Press.

Galaway, Burt, and Joe Hudson
1996 Restorative Justice: International Perspectives. Monsey, NY: Criminal Justice Press.

Gannett, Lisa
2004 The Biological Reification of Race. British Journal for the Philosophy of Science 55:323–345.

Garroutte, Eva Marie
2003 Real Indians: Identity and the Survival of Native America. Berkeley: University of California Press.

Garth, Bryant G., and Austin Sarat
1998 Justice and Power in Sociolegal Studies. Evanston, IL: Northwestern University Press and the American Bar Foundation.

Gibbons, Ann
1996 DNA Enters Dust up over Bones. Science 274(5285):172.

Gluckman, Max
1955 Judicial Process among the Barotse of Northern Rhodesia. Manchester: Manchester University Press.

Goffman, Erving
1961   The Characteristics of Total Institutions. *In* Complex Organizations: A
        Sociological Reader. A. Etzioni, ed. Pp. 313–314. New York: Holt, Rine-
        hart, and Winston.

Gooding, Susan Staiger
1994   Place, Race, and Names: Layered Identities in *United States v. Oregon*,
        Confederated Tribes of the Colville Reservation. Law & Society Review
        28(5):1181–1229.

Gooding, Susan Staiger, and Eve Darian-Smith
2001   Putting Law in Its Place in Native North America: Introduction to the
        Symposium. PoLAR: Political and Legal Anthropology Review 24(2):1–
        8.

Gordon, Avery, and Christopher Newfield
1996   Mapping Multiculturalism. Minneapolis: University of Minnesota Press.

Gould, Stephen Jay
1996   The Mismeasure of Man. New York: Norton.

Graves, Joseph L.
2001   The Emperor's New Clothes: Biological Theories of Race at the Millen-
        nium. New Brunswick, NJ: Rutgers University Press.

Gray-Kanatiiosh, Barbara A., and Pat Lauderdale
2006   The Web of Justice: Restorative Justice Has Presented Only Part of the
        Story. Wicazo Sa Review 21(1):29–41.

Green, Ross Gordon
1998   Justice in Aboriginal Communities: Sentencing Alternatives. Saskatoon,
        SK: Purich Publishing.

Greenfeld, Lawrence A., and Steven K. Smith
1999   American Indians and Crime. Washington: Bureau of Justice Statistics,
        US Department of Justice.

Gross, Ariela J.
1998   Litigating Whiteness: Trials of Racial Determination in the Nineteenth-
        Century South. The Yale Law Journal 108(1):109–188.

Guenther, Mathias
2006   Discussion: The Concept of Indigeneity. Social Anthropology 14(1):17–
        19.

Guerrero, M. A. Jaimes
2003   Global Genocide and Biocolonialism: On the Effect of the Human Genome
        Diversity Project on Targeted Indigenous Peoples/Ecocultures as "Isolates
        of Historic Interest." *In* Violence and the Body: Race, Gender, and the State.
        A. J. Aldama, ed. Pp. 171–188. Bloomington: Indiana University Press.

Guest, James J. R.
1999   Aboriginal Legal Theory and Restorative Justice. Justice as Healing
        4(1):7–8.

Gupta, Akhil, and James Ferguson
1997   Discipline and Practice: "The Field" As Site, Method, and Location in
        Anthropology. *In* Anthropological Locations: Boundaries and Grounds
        of a Field Science. A. Gupta and J. Ferguson, eds. Pp. 1–46. Berkeley:
        University of California Press.

Gutmann, Amy
1994   Multiculturalism. Princeton: Princeton University Press.

Haberfeld, Steven, and Jon Townsend
1993   Power and Dispute Resolution in Indian Country. Mediation Quarterly
        10(4):405–422.

Haller, John S.
1971   Race and the Concept of Progress in Nineteenth Century American Eth-
        nology. American Anthropologist 73(3):710–724.

Hamilton, Jennifer A.
2008a   Revitalizing Difference in the HapMap: Race, Biomedicine, and Contem-
        porary Human Genetic Variation Research. The Journal of Law, Medi-
        cine & Ethics 36(3).
2008b   The Case of the Genetic Ancestor: DNA Ancestry Tracing, Legal Subjec-
        tivity and Race in America. Paper presented at the DNA, Race, and His-
        tory Conference, Center for Race and Ethnicity, Rutgers University, April
        18–19, in New Brunswick, NJ.

Haraway, Donna J.
1997   Modest_Witness@Second_Millennium.Femaleman©_Meets_Onco-
        mouse™. New York: Routledge.

Harding, Sarah
2005   *Bonnichsen v. United States*: Time, Place, and the Search for Identity.
        International Journal of Cultural Property 12(2):15.

Harper, Kenn
2001   Give Me My Father's Body: The Life of Minik, the New York Eskimo.
        New York: Pocket Books.

Harring, Sidney L.
1994   Crow Dog's Case: American Indian Sovereignty, Tribal Law, and United
        States Law in the Nineteenth Century. Cambridge and New York: Cam-
        bridge University Press.
1998   White Man's Law: Native People in Nineteenth-Century Canadian Juris-
        prudence. Toronto and Buffalo: University of Toronto Press.

Harris, Cole
1997   The Resettlement of British Columbia: Essays on Colonialism and
        Geographical Change. Vancouver: University of British Columbia
        Press.
2002   Making Native Space: Colonialism, Resistance, and Reserves in British
        Columbia. Vancouver: University of British Columbia Press.

Harris, Cheryl I.
1993   Whiteness as Property. Harvard Law Review 106:1709–1791.

Harry, Debra
2002   The Human Genome Diversity Project: Implications for Indigenous Peoples. *In* An Introduction to Women's Studies: Gender in a Transnational World. I. Grewal and C. Kaplan, eds. Pp. 125–128. Boston: McGraw-Hill.

Harry, Debra, Stephanie Howard, and Brett Lee Shelton
2000   Indigenous People, Genes and Genetics: What Indigenous People Should Know About Biocolonialism. Pp. 1–41. Wadsworth, NV: Indigenous Peoples Council on Biocolonialism.

Havemann, Paul
1988   The Indigensation of Social Control in Canada. *In* Indigenous Law and the State. B. Morse and G. Woodman, eds. Dordrecht: Foris Publishing.

Hazlehurst, Kayleen M.
1994   A Healing Place: Indigenous Visions for Personal Empowerment and Community Recovery. Rockhampton, Qld., Australia: Central Queensland University Press.
1995a   Legal Pluralism and the Colonial Legacy: Indigenous Experiences of Justice in Canada, Australia, and New Zealand. Aldershot and Brookfield USA: Avebury.
1995b   Perceptions of Justice: Issues in Indigenous and Community Empowerment. Aldershot and Brookfield USA: Avebury.

Hibbert, Michelle
1998/99 Galileos or Grave Robbers? Science, the Native American Graves Protection and Repatriation Act, and the First Amendment. American Indian Law Review 23:425–458.

Highet, Megan
2005   Body Snatching & Grave Robbing: Bodies for Science. History and Anthropology 16(4):26.

Hirsch, Eric, and Michael O'Hanlon
1995   The Anthropology of Landscape: Perspectives on Place and Space. Oxford: Oxford University Press.

Hirsch, Susan F.
1998   Pronouncing & Persevering: Gender and the Discourses of Disputing in an African Islamic Court. Chicago: University of Chicago Press.

Hitt, Jack
2005   Mighty White of You: Racial Preferences Color America's Oldest Skulls and Bones. Harper's Magazine 311(1862):39–55.

Hobsbawm, Eric, and Terence Ranger
1983   The Invention of Tradition. Cambridge: Cambridge University Press.

Huber, Marg
1993   Mediation around the Medicine Wheel. Mediation Quarterly 10(4):355–365.

Huhndorf, Shari M.
2001   Going Native: Indians in the American Cultural Imagination. Ithaca, NY: Cornell University Press.

Humphrey, Caroline, and Katherine Verdery
2004   Introduction: Raising Questions about Property. *In* Property in Question: Value Transformation in the Global Economy. K. Verdery and C. Humphrey, eds. Pp. 1–25. Oxford and New York: Berg.

Hylton, John H.
1995   Social Policy and Canada's Aboriginal People: The Need for Fundamental Reforms. *In* Popular Justice and Community Regeneration: Pathways of Indigenous Reform. K. M. Hazlehurst, ed. Pp. 3–20. Westport, CN: Praeger.

Jack, Agnes
2006   Behind Closed Doors: Stories from the Kamloops Indian Residential School. Penticton, BC: Theytus Books.

Jackson, Jean
1995   Culture, Genuine and Spurious: The Politics of Indianness in the Vaupes, Colombia. American Ethnologist 22:3–28.

Jain, Sarah S. Lochlann
2004   "Dangerous Instrumentality": The Bystander as Subject in Automobility. Cultural Anthropology 19(1):61–94.

James, Rudy
1997   Devilfish Bay: The Giant Devilfish Story. Woodinville, WA: Wolfhouse Publishing.

Johansen, Bruce E.
2004   Kennewick Man: The Facts, the Fantasies, and the Stakes. *In* Enduring Legacies: Native American Treaties and Contemporary Controversies. B. E. Johansen, ed. Westport, CN: Praeger.

Johnston, Josephine
2003   Resisting a Genetic Identity: The Black Seminoles and Genetic Tests of Ancestry. The Journal of Law, Medicine & Ethics 31(2):262–271.

Jones, Peter, and Darby Stapp
2003   An Anthropological Perspective on Magistrate Jelderks' Kennewick Man Decision. High Plains Applied Anthropologist 23(1):1–16.

Kauanui, J. Kehaulani
2002   The Politics of Blood and Sovereignty in *Rice v. Cayetano*. PoLAR: Political and Legal Anthropology Review 25(1):110–128.

Keesing, Roger M.
1992   Custom and Confrontation: The Kwaio Struggle for Cultural Autonomy. Chicago: University of Chicago Press.

Kehoe, Alice Beck
1998   The Land of Prehistory: A Critical History of American Archaeology. New York: Routledge.

Kelm, Mary-Ellen
1998   Colonizing Bodies: Aboriginal Health and Healing in British Columbia, 1900–50. Vancouver: University of British Columbia Press.

Kerber, Jordan E.
2006   Cross-Cultural Collaboration: Native Peoples and Archaeology in the
         Northeastern United States. Lincoln: University of Nebraska Press.

Kesselman, Jonathan R.
2000   Aboriginal Taxation of Non-Aboriginal Residents: Representation, Dis-
         crimination, and Accountability in the Context of First Nations Auton-
         omy. http://www.arts.ubc.ca/cresp/fntax.pdf (accessed January 3, 2004).

Kirsch, Stuart
2001   Lost Worlds: Environmental Disaster, "Culture Loss," and the Law. Cur-
         rent Anthropology 42(2):167–178.

Knafla, Louis A.
1986   Law & Justice in a New Land: Essays in Western Canadian Legal His-
         tory. Toronto: Carswell.

Knafla, Louis A., and Jonathan Scott Swainger
2005   Laws and Societies in the Canadian Prairie West, 1670–1940. Vancouver:
         University of British Columbia Press.

Knight, Rolf
1996   Indians at Work: An Informal History of Native Labour in British Colum-
         bia, 1848–1930. Vancouver: New Star Books.

Kuper, Adam
2003   The Return of the Native. Current Anthropology 44(3):389–402.

Lambertson, Ross
1995   After *Union Colliery*: Law, Race, and Class in the Coalmines of British
         Columbia. *In* Essays in the History of Canadian Law: British Columbia
         and the Yukon. Vol. IV. H. Foster and J. McLaren, eds. Pp. 386–422.
         Toronto and Buffalo: University of Toronto Press.

Landzelius, Kyra
2006   Native on the Net: Indigenous and Diasporic Peoples in the Virtual Age.
         Abingdon and New York: Routledge.

LaRocque, Emma
1997   Re-Examining Culturally Appropriate Models in Criminal Justice Appli-
         cations. *In* Aboriginal and Treaty Rights in Canada: Essays on Law,
         Equity, and Respect for Difference. M. Asch, ed. Pp. 75–96. Vancouver:
         University of British Columbia Press.

LaVaque-Manty, Danielle
2000   There Are Indians in the Museum of Natural History. Wicazo Sa Review
         15(1):71–89.

Lazarus-Black, Mindie
1994   Legitimate Acts and Illegal Encounters: Law and Society in Antigua and
         Barbuda. Washington: Smithsonian Institution Press.

Lazarus-Black, Mindie, and Susan F. Hirsch
1994   Contested States: Law, Hegemony and Resistance. New York: Rout-
         ledge.

Lee, G.
1997   The Newest Old Gem: Family Group Conferencing. Justice as Healing 2:2.

Lee, Richard B.
2006   Twenty-First Century Indigenism. Anthropological Theory 6(4):455–479.

Lemonick, Michael D., and Andrea Dorfman
2006   Who Were the First Americans? Time Magazine 167(11):44–52.

Lepper, Bradley T., and Robson Bonnichsen
2004   New Perspectives on the First Americans. College Station, TX: Center for the Study of the First Americans.

LeResche, Diane
1993   The Reawakening of Sacred Justice. Clearinghouse Review 27(8):893–899.

Li, Tania Murray
2000   Articulating Indigenous Identity in Indonesia: Resource Politics and the Tribal Slot. Comparative Studies in Society and History 42(1):31.

Lieberman, Leonard
2001   How "Caucasoids" Got Such Big Crania and Why They Shrank: From Morton to Rushton. Current Anthropology 42(1):28.

Lindee, M. Susan, Alan H. Goodman, and Deborah Heath
2003   Anthropology in an Age of Genetics: Practice, Discourse, and Critique. *In* Genetic Nature/Culture: Anthropology and Science Beyond the Two-Culture Divide. A. H. Goodman, D. Heath, and M. S. Lindee, eds. Pp. 1–19. Berkeley: University of California Press.

Linden, Rick, and Don Clairmont
1998   Making It Work: Planning and Evaluating Community Corrections & Healing Projects in Aboriginal Communities. Ottawa: Solicitor General Canada.

Llewellyn, K. N., and E. Adamson Hoebel
1941   The Cheyenne Way: Conflict and Case Law in Primitive Jurisprudence. Norman: University of Oklahoma Press.

Lock, Margaret
1999   Genetic Diversity and the Politics of Difference. Chicago-Kent Law Review 75:83–111.

Loo, Tina
1994   The Road from Bute Inlet: Crime and Colonial Identity in British Columbia. *In* Essays in the History of Canadian Law: Crime and Criminal Justice. Vol. V. J. Phillips, T. Loo, and S. Lewthwaite, eds. Pp. 112–142. Toronto: University of Toronto Press.
1995   Tonto's Due: Law, Culture, and Colonization in British Columbia. *In* Essays in the History of Canadian Law VI: British Columbia and the Yukon. H. Foster and J. McLaren, eds. Pp. 128–170. Toronto and Buffalo: University of Toronto Press.

114   *Bibliography*

López, Ian F. Haney
1996   White by Law: The Legal Construction of Race. New York: New York University Press.

Lujan, Carol Chiago, and Gordon Adams
2004   US Colonization of Indian Justice Systems: A Brief History. Wicazo Sa Review 19(2):9–23.

Lynch, Michael, and Steve Woolgar
1990   Representation in Scientific Practice. Cambridge, MA: MIT Press.

Mackey, Eva
1999   The House of Difference: Cultural Politics and National Identity in Canada. London and New York: Routledge.

Macklem, Patrick
2001   Indigenous Difference and the Constitution of Canada. Toronto and Buffalo: University of Toronto Press.

Manitoba
1991a   Report of the Aboriginal Justice Inquiry of Manitoba: The Justice System and Aboriginal People. Winnipeg: Queen's Printer.
1991b   Report of the Aboriginal Justice Inquiry of Manitoba: The Deaths of Helen Betty Osborne and John Joseph Harper. Winnipeg: Queen's Printer.

Marks, Jonathan
2001a   Scientific and Folk Ideas about Heredity. *In* The Human Genome Project and Minority Communities: Ethical, Social, and Political Dilemmas. R. A. Zilinskas and P. J. Balint, eds. Pp. 53–66. Westport, CN: Praeger.
2001b   "We're Going to Tell These People Who They Really Are": Science and Relatedness. *In* Relative Values: Reconfiguring Kinship Studies. S. Franklin and S. McKinnon, eds. Pp. 355–383. Durham: Duke University Press.
2002   What It Means to Be 98% Chimpanzee: Apes, People, and Their Genes. Berkeley: University of California Press.
2005   Your Body, My Property: The Problem of Colonial Genetics in a Post-Colonial World. *In* Embedding Ethics. L. Meskell and P. Pels, eds. Pp. 29–45. Oxford and New York: Berg.

Matoesian, Gregory M.
1993   Reproducing Rape: Domination through Talk in the Courtroom. Cambridge, UK: Polity Press.

Matsuda, Mari J.
1988   Native Custom and Official Law in Hawaii. Internationales Jahrbuch für Rechtsanthropologie 3:135–146.

Maurer, Bill, and Sally Merry
1997   Gender, Violence, and the Law. *In* PoLAR: Political and Legal Anthropology Review. Vol. 20 (2).

Mawani, Renisa
2002   In Between and Out of Place: Mixed-Race Identity, Liquor, and the Law in British Columbia, 1850–1913. *In* Race, Space, and the Law:

Unmapping a White Settler Society. S. Razack, ed. Pp. 47–70. Toronto: Between the Lines.
2003   Imperial Legacies (Post)Colonial Identities: Law, Space and the Making of Stanley Park. Law/Text/Culture 7:98–141.

Maybury-Lewis, David
2002   Indigenous Peoples, Ethnic Groups, and the State. Boston: Allyn and Bacon.

McGillivray, Anne, and Brenda Comaskey
1999   Black Eyes All of the Time: Intimate Violence, Aboriginal Women, and the Justice System. Toronto: University of Toronto Press.

McLaren, John, Hamar Foster, and Chet Orloff
1992   Law for the Elephant, Law for the Beaver: Essays in the Legal History of the North American West. Regina, SK and Pasadena, CA: Canadian Plains Research Center, University of Regina & Ninth Judicial Circuit Historical Society.

McNamara, L.
1995   Aboriginal Justice Reform in Canada: Alternatives to State Control. *In* Perceptions of Justice: Issues of Indigenous Community Empowerment. K. Hazlehurst, ed. Aldershot: Avebury.

Melton, Ada Pecos
1995   Indigenous Justice Systems and Tribal Society. Juridicature 79(3):126–133.

Menkel-Meadow, Carrie
2007   Restorative Justice: What Is It and Does It Work? Annual Review of Law and Social Science 3(1):161–187.

Merry, Sally Engle
2000   Colonizing Hawai'i: The Cultural Power of Law. Princeton: Princeton University Press.

Meyer, Melissa L.
1999   American Indian Blood Quantum Requirements: Blood Is Thicker Than Family. *In* Over the Edge: Remapping the American West. V. J. Matsumoto and B. Allmendinger, eds. Pp. 231–252. Berkeley: University of California Press.

Mihesuah, Devon A.
2000   Repatriation Reader: Who Owns American Indian Remains? Lincoln: University of Nebraska Press.

Miller, Bruce G.
1998   Culture as Cultural Defense: An American Indian Sacred Site in Court. American Indian Quarterly 22(1 & 2):83–97.
2001   The Problem of Justice: Tradition and Law in the Coast Salish World. Lincoln: University of Nebraska Press.
2003a   Justice, Law, and the Lens of Culture. Wicazo Sa Review 18(2):135–149.
2003b   Invisible Indigenes: The Politics of Nonrecognition. Lincoln: University of Nebraska Press.

Milloy, John Sheridan
1999   A National Crime: The Canadian Government and the Residential School System, 1879 to 1986. Winnipeg: University of Manitoba Press.

Milun, Kathryn
2001   Keeping-While-Giving-Back: Computer Imaging and Native American Repatriation. PoLAR: Political and Legal Anthropology Review 24(2):39–57.

Minow, Martha
1995   Rights and Cultural Difference. *In* Identities, Politics, and Rights. A. Sarat and T. R. Kearns, eds. Pp. 347–365. Ann Arbor: University of Michigan Press.

Minthorn, Armand
1996   Human Remains Should Be Reburied. http://www.umatilla.nsn.us/kman1.html (accessed March 18, 2008).

Monture-Angus, Patricia A.
1996   Lessons in Decolonization: Aboriginal Overrepresentation in Canadian Criminal Justice. *In* Visions of the Heart: Canadian Aboriginal Issues. D. A. Long and O. P. Dickason, eds. Pp. 335–354. Toronto and Fort Worth: Harcourt Brace & Company Canada.

Monture-OKanee, Patricia
1992   The Violence We Women Do: A First Nations View. *In* Challenging Times: The Women's Movement in Canada and the United States. D. H. Flaherty and C. Backhouse, eds. Montreal: McGill-Queen's University Press.

Moodley, Kogila
1983   Canadian Multiculturalism as Ideology. Ethnic and Racial Studies 6(3):322–331.

Moore, Sally Falk
1978   Law as Process: An Anthropological Approach. London and Boston: Routledge.
1986   Social Facts and Fabrications: "Customary" Law on Kilimanjaro, 1880-1980. Cambridge and New York: Cambridge University Press.

Muckle, Robert J.
1998   The First Nations of British Columbia: An Anthropological Survey. Vancouver: University of British Columbia Press.

Murray, Virginia
1998   A Comparative Survey of the Historic Civil, Common and American Indian Tribal Law Responses to Domestic Violence. Oklahoma City University Law Review 23(1 & 2):433–457.

Musqueam Indian Band
1989   The UEL Park and the Musqueam Band. Pp. 1–4. Vancouver: Musqueam Indian Band.

Musselman, Jenna
2005   Ninth Circuit Limits NAGPRA to Remains Linked with Presently Existing Tribes. Ecology Law Quarterly 32:707–713.

Nadasdy, Paul
2002   "Property" and Aboriginal Land Claims in the Canadian Subarctic: Some Theoretical Considerations. American Anthropologist 104(1):247–261.

Nader, Laura
1990   Harmony Ideology: Justice and Control in a Zapotec Mountain Village. Stanford: Stanford University Press.
2002   The Life of the Law: Anthropological Projects. Berkeley: University of California Press.

Nader, Laura, and Harry F. Todd Jr.
1978   The Disputing Process: Law in Ten Societies. New York: Columbia University Press.

Nahanee, Teressa
1993   Dancing with a Gorilla: Aboriginal Women, Justice and the Charter. *In* Aboriginal Peoples and the Justice System: Report of the National Round Table on Aboriginal Justice Issues. R. C. o. A. Peoples, ed. Ottawa: Minister of Supply and Services Canada.

Nielsen, Marianne O.
1991   Criminal Justice and Native Self-Government in Canada: Is Incorporation of Traditional Justice Practices Feasible? Law and Anthropology 6:7–24.

Norgren, Jill, and Serena Nanda
1996   American Cultural Pluralism and Law. Westport, CN: Praeger.

O'Connell, Karen
2007   "We Who Are Not Here": Law, Whiteness, Indigenous Peoples and the Promise of Genetic Identification. International Journal of Law in Context 3(1):35–58.

O'Donnell, Marg
1995   Mediation within Aboriginal Communities: Issues and Challenges. *In* Popular Justice and Community Regeneration: Pathways of Indigenous Reform. K. M. Hazlehurst, ed. Pp. 89–102. Westport, CN: Praeger.

Okin, Susan Moller, Joshua Cohen, Matthew Howard, and Martha C. Nussbaum.
1999   Is Multiculturalism Bad for Women? Princeton: Princeton University Press.

Olund, Eric N.
2002   From Savage Space to Governable Space: The Extension of United States Judicial Sovereignty over Indian Country in the Nineteenth Century. Cultural Geographies 9:129–157.

Parfit, Michael, and Kenneth Garrett
2000   Hunt for the First Americans. National Geographic 198(6):40–67.

Parry, Susan, and Carl Elliott
2002   Genetic Ancestry Tracing and American Indian Identity. American Philo-
         sophical Association Newsletter 1(2):9–12.

Pensley, D. S.
2005   The Native American Graves Protection and Repatriation Act (1990):
         Where the Native Voice Is Missing. Wicazo Sa Review 20(2):37–64.

Perry, Adele
2001   On the Edge of Empire: Gender, Race, and the Making of British Colum-
         bia, 1849–1871. Toronto: University of Toronto Press.

Perry, Richard Warren
2002   Commentary: Remapping the Legal Landscapes of Native North Amer-
         ica: Layered Identities in Comparative Perspective. PoLAR: Political and
         Legal Anthropology Review 25(1):129–150.
2006   Native American Tribal Gaming as Crime against Nature. PoLAR: Politi-
         cal and Legal Anthropology Review 29(1):110–131.

Porter, Robert B.
1997   Strengthening Tribal Sovereignty through Peacemaking: How the Anglo-
         American Legal Tradition Destroys Indigenous Societies. Columbia
         Human Rights Review 28(2):235–305.

Pospisil, Leopold J.
1958   Kapauku Papuans and Their Law. New Haven: Dept. of Anthropology,
         Yale University.

Povinelli, Elizabeth A.
2002a   The Cunning of Recognition: Indigenous Alterities and the Making of
         Australian Multiculturalism. Durham: Duke University Press.
2002b   Notes on Gridlock: Genealogy, Intimacy, Sexuality. Public Culture
         14(1):215–238.
2004   At Home in the Violence of Recognition. *In* Property in Question: Value
         Transformation in the Global Economy. K. Verdery and C. Humphrey,
         eds. Pp. 185–206. Oxford and New York: Berg.

Preston, Douglas
1997   The Lost Man. The New Yorker 73(16):70–81.
1998   Skin & Bones. The New Yorker 73(46):52–53.

Prucha, Francis Paul
1982   Indian Policy in the United States: Historical Essays. Lincoln: University
         of Nebraska Press.

Ramos, Alcida Rita
1998   Indigenism: Ethnic Politics in Brazil. Madison: University of Wisconsin Press.

Rawson & Wiles Ltd.
1967   A Development Plan for Musqueam Indian Reserves 2 & 3. Vancouver:
         Rawson & Wiles Ltd.

Ray, S. Alan
2006   Native American Identity and the Challenge of Kennewick Man. Temple Law Review 79:89–154.

Razack, Sherene
1998   Looking White People in the Eye: Gender, Race, and Culture in Courtrooms and Classrooms. Toronto and Buffalo: University of Toronto Press.
1999   Making Canada White: Law and the Policing of Bodies of Colour in the 1990s. Canadian Journal of Law & Society 14(1):159–184.
2002a   Gendered Racial Violence and Spatialized Justice: The Murder of Pamela George. *In* Race, Space, and the Law: Unmapping a White Settler Society. S. Razack, ed. Pp. 121–156. Toronto: Between the Lines.
2002b   Introduction: When Place Becomes Race. *In* Race, Space, and the Law: Unmapping a White Settler Society. S. Razack, ed. Pp. 1–20. Toronto: Between the Lines.
2002c   Race, Space, and the Law: Unmapping a White Settler Society. Toronto: Between the Lines.

Reardon, Jenny
2004   Decoding Race and Human Difference in a Genomic Age. Differences 15(3):38–65.
2005   Race to the Finish: Identity and Governance in an Age of Genomics. Princeton: Princeton University Press.

Reichs, Kathy
1998   Forensic Osteology: Advances in the Identification of Human Remains. Springfield, IL: Charles C. Thomas.

Richland, Justin B.
2007   Pragmatic Paradoxes and Ironies of Indigeneity at the "Edge" of Hopi Sovereignty. American Ethnologist 34(3):540–557.

Riding In, James
1992   Six Pawnee Crania: Historical and Contemporary Issues Associated with the Massacre and Decapitation of Pawnee Indians in 1869. American Indian Culture and Research Journal 16(2):101–119.
2002   *The United States v Yellow Sun et al* (the Pawnee People): A Case Study of Institutional and Societal Racism and US Justice in Nebraska from the 1850s to 1870s. Wicazo Sa Review 17(1):13–41.

Riding In, James, Cal Seciwa, Suzan Shown Harjo, Walter R. Echo-Hawk, and Rebecca Tsosie
2004   Protecting Native American Human Remains, Burial Grounds, and Sacred Places: Panel Discussion. Wicazo Sa Review 19(2):169–183.

Ripley, Will R.
2005   You're Not Native American--You're Too Old!: *Bonnichsen v. United States* Exposes the Native American Graves Protection and Repatriation Act. Journal of Gender, Race and Justice 9:137–160.

Robbins, Rebecca L.
1992   Self-Determination and Subordination: The Past, Present, and Future of American Indian Governance. *In* The State of Native America: Genocide, Colonization, and Resistance. M. A. Jaimes, ed. Pp. 87–121. Boston: South End Press.

Rohrer, Judy
2006   "Got Race?" The Production of Haole and the Distortion of Indigeneity in the *Rice* Decision. Contemporary Pacific 18(1):1–31.

Rose, Carol M.
1994   Property and Persuasion: Essays on the History, Theory, and Rhetoric of Ownership. Boulder, CO: Westview Press.

Rose, Jerome C., Thomas J. Green, and Victoria D. Green
1996   NAGPRA Is Forever: Osteology and the Repatriation of Skeletons. Annual Review of Anthropology 25:24.

Rose, Nikolas
2007   The Politics of Life Itself: Biomedicine, Power, and Subjectivity in the Twenty-First Century. Princeton: Princeton University Press.

Ross, Luana
1998   Inventing the Savage: The Social Construction of Native American Criminality. Austin: University of Texas Press.

Ross, Rupert
1996   Returning to the Teachings: Exploring Aboriginal Justice. Toronto: Penguin Books.

Roy, Patricia
1989   A White Man's Province: British Columbia Politicians and Chinese and Japanese Immigrants, 1858–1914. Vancouver: University of British Columbia Press.

Royal Commission on Aboriginal Peoples
1996   Bridging the Cultural Divide: A Report on Aboriginal People and Criminal Justice in Canada. Ottawa: Minister of Supply and Services Canada.

Ryan, Joan
1995   Doing Things the Right Way: Dene Traditional Justice in Lac La Martre, NWT. Calgary: University of Calgary Press.

Said, Edward
1978   Orientalism. New York: Vintage Books.

Samson, Colin
2001   Rights as the Reward for Simulated Cultural Sameness: The Innu in the Canadian Colonial Context. *In* Culture and Rights: Anthropological Perspectives. J. K. Cowan, M.-B. Dembour, and R. A. Wilson, eds. Pp. 226–248. Cambridge and New York: Cambridge University Press.

Sangster, Joan
2002   "She Is Hostile to Our Ways": First Nations Girls Sentenced to the Ontario Training School for Girls, 1933–1960. http://www.historycooperative. org/journals/lhr/20.1/sangster.html (accessed February 21, 2002).

Santos, Ricardo Ventura
2003   Indigenous People, Changing Social and Political Landscapes, and Human Genetics in Amazonia. *In* Genetic Nature/Culture: Anthropology and

Science Beyond the Two-Culture Divide. A. H. Goodman, D. Heath, and M. S. Lindee, eds. Pp. 23–40. Berkeley: University of California Press.

Sarat, Austin, and Thomas R. Kearns
1995   Identities, Politics, and Rights. Ann Arbor: University of Michigan Press.
1999   Cultural Pluralism, Identity Politics, and the Law. Ann Arbor: University of Michigan Press.

Schick, Carol
2002   Keeping the Ivory Tower White: Discourses of Racial Domination. *In* Race, Space, and the Law: Unmapping a White Settler Society. S. Razack, ed. Pp. 99–120. Toronto: Between the Lines.

Seed, Patricia
2001   American Pentimento: The Invention of Indians and the Pursuit of Riches. Minneapolis: University of Minnesota Press.

Sierra, Maria Teresa
1995   Indian Rights and Customary Law in Mexico: A Study of the Nahuas in the Sierra De Puebla. Law and Society Review 29(2):227–254.
2005   The Revival of Indigenous Justice in Mexico: Challenges for Human Rights and the State. PoLAR: Political and Legal Anthropology Review 28(1):52–72.

Slayman, Andrew L.
1997   Special Report: A Battle over Bones. Archaeology 50(1):8.

Smedley, Audrey
1999   Race in North America: Origin and Evolution of a Worldview. Boulder, CO: Westview Press.
2006   On the Confusion of "Race" With Biophysical Diversity. American Psychologist 61(2):180–181.

Smedley, Audrey, and Brian D. Smedley
2005   Race as Biology Is Fiction, Racism as a Social Problem Is Real: Anthropological and Historical Perspectives on the Social Construction of Race. American Psychologist 60(1):16–26.

Smith, Andrea
2005   Conquest: Sexual Violence and American Indian Genocide. Cambridge, MA: South End Press.

Smith, David Glenn, Ripan S. Malhi, Jason A. Eshleman, and Frederika A. Kaestle
2000   Report on DNA Analysis of the Remains Of "Kennewick Man" From Columbia Park, Washington. http://www.nps.gov/archeology/kennewick/smith.htm (accessed March 13, 2008).

Snyder, Francis G.
1981   Colonialism and Legal Form: The Creation of "Customary Law" In Senegal. Journal of Legal Pluralism and Unofficial Law 9:49–90.

Sommer, Marianne
2006   Mirror, Mirror on the Wall: Neanderthal as Image and "Distortion" In Early 20th-Century French Science and Press. Social Studies of Science 36(2):207–240.

2007   Bones and Ochre: The Curious Afterlife of the Red Lady of Paviland. Cambridge, MA: Harvard University Press.

Spivak, Gayatri Chakravorty
1987   In Other Worlds: Essays in Cultural Politics. New York: Methuen.

Spruhan, Paul
2006   A Legal History of Blood Quantum in Federal Indian Law to 1935. South Dakota Law Review 51:1–50.

Starr, June, and Jane Fishburne Collier
1989   History and Power in the Study of Law: New Directions in Legal Anthropology. Ithaca, NY: Cornell University Press.

Stevenson, Winona
1995   Post-Colonial Reflections on the Past and Future Paths of Canadian Aboriginal Women (or, out from under the Skirts of Her Majesty). London Journal of Canadian Studies 11:1–27.
1999   Colonialism and First Nations Women in Canada. *In* Scratching the Surface: Canadian, Anti-Racist, Feminist Thought. E. Dua and A. Robertson, eds. Pp. 49–80. Toronto: Women's Press.

Stocking, George W.
1988   Bones, Bodies, Behavior: Essays on Biological Anthropology. Madison: University of Wisconsin Press.

Strang, Heather, and John Braithwaite
2000   Restorative Justice: Philosophy to Practice. Aldershot: Ashgate.
2002   Restorative Justice and Family Violence. Cambridge and New York: Cambridge University Press.

Sturm, Circe
2002   Blood Politics: Race, Culture, and Identity in the Cherokee Nation of Oklahoma. Berkeley: University of California Press.

TallBear, Kimberly
2001   Racializing Tribal Identity and the Implications for Political and Institutional Development. *In* Indigenous Peoples, Racism and the United Nations. M. N. Nakata, ed. Pp. 163–174. Altona, Victoria: Common Ground Publishing.
2003   DNA, Blood, and Racializing the Tribe. Wicazo Sa Review 18(1):81–107.
2007   Narratives of Race and Indigeneity in the Genographic Project. The Journal of Law, Medicine & Ethics 35(3):412–424.

Tauri, Juan Marcellus
1998   Family Group Conferencing: A Case Study of the Indigenisation of New Zealand's Justice System. Current Issues in Criminal Justice 10(2):168–182.
1999   Family Group Conferencing: The Myth of Indigenous Empowerment in New Zealand. Justice as Healing 4(1):1–5.

Taylor, Charles
1994   The Politics of Recognition. *In* Multiculturalism. A. Gutmann, ed. Pp. 25–73. Princeton: Princeton University Press.

Taylor, Graham D.
1980   The New Deal and American Indian Tribalism: The Administration of the Indian Reorganization Act, 1934–45. Lincoln: University of Nebraska Press.

Tennant, Paul
1990   Aboriginal Peoples and Politics: The Indian Land Question in British Columbia, 1849–1989. Vancouver: University of British Columbia Press.

Thomas, David Hurst
2000   Skull Wars: Kennewick Man, Archaeology, and the Battle for Native American Identity. New York: Basic Books.

Torres, Gerald, and Kathryn Milun
1995   Translating *Yonnondio* by Precedent and Evidence: The Mashpee Indian Case. *In* Critical Race Theory: The Cutting Edge. R. Delgado, ed. Pp. 48–55. Philadelphia: Temple University Press.

Trigger, Bruce G.
1980   Archaeology and the Image of the American Indian. American Antiquity 45(4):662–676.
2003   Artifacts & Ideas: Essays in Archaeology. New Brunswick, NJ: Transaction Publishers.

Trope, Jack F., and Walter R. Echohawk
1998   The Native American Graves Protection and Repatriation Act: Background and Legislative History. *In* Readings in American Indian Law: Recalling the Rhythm of Survival. J. Carrillo, ed. Pp. 178–187. Philadelphia: Temple University Press.

Tsosie, Rebecca
1999   Privileging Claims to the Past: Ancient Human Remains and Contemporary Cultural Values. Arizona State Law Journal 31(2):583–677.
2005   The New Challenge to Native Identity: An Essay on "Indigeneity" and "Whiteness." Washington University Journal of Law and Policy 18:55–98.

Turner, Trudy
2005   Biological Anthropology and Ethics: From Repatriation to Genetic Identity. Albany: State University of New York Press.

Turner Strong, Pauline, and Barrik Van Winkle
1996   "Indian Blood": Reflections on the Reckoning and Refiguring of Native North American Identity. Cultural Anthropology 11(4):30.

Valencia-Weber, Gloria
1994   Tribal Courts: Custom and Innovative Law. New Mexico Law Review 24(2):225–263.

Van Biema, David
1994   The Banishing Judge. Time 144(11):74.

VARJP
n.d.   The Vancouver Aboriginal Restorative Justice Program. Pp. 1–4. Unpublished report on file with author.

Verdery, Katherine, and Caroline Humphrey
2004   Property in Question: Value Transformation in the Global Economy. Oxford and New York: Berg.

Wald, Priscilla
2006   Blood and Stories: How Genomics Is Rewriting Race, Medicine and Human History. Patterns of Prejudice 40(4):303 - 333.

Walker, Cheryl
1997   Indian Nation: Native American Literature and Nineteenth-Century Nationalisms. Durham: Duke University Press.

Ward, W. Peter
1990   White Canada Forever: Popular Attitudes and Public Policy toward Orientals in British Columbia. Montreal: McGill-Queen's University Press.

Warhaft, E. Barry, Ted Palys, and Wilma Boyce
1999   "This Is How We Did It": One Canadian First Nation Community's Effort to Achieve Aboriginal Justice. The Australian and New Zealand Journal of Criminology 32(2):168–181.

Warry, Wayne
1998   Unfinished Dreams: Community Healing and the Reality of Aboriginal Self -Government. Toronto and Buffalo: University of Toronto Press.

Watkins, Joe
2000   Indigenous Archaeology: American Indian Values and Scientific Practice. Walnut Creek, CA: Alta Mira Press.
2004   Becoming American or Becoming Indian?: NAGPRA, Kennewick and Cultural Affiliation. Journal of Social Archaeology 4(1):60–80.
2005   Through Wary Eyes: Indigenous Perspectives on Archaeology. Annual Review of Anthropology 34(1):429–449.

Weaver, Jace
2000   Indigenousness and Indigeneity. *In* A Companion to Postcolonial Studies. H. Schwarz and S. Ray, eds. Pp. 221–235. Malden, MA: Blackwell Publishers.

Weightman, Barbara
1972   Musqueam Reserve. PhD diss. University of Washington.

Whitt, Laurie Anne
1998   Biocolonialism and the Commodification of Knowledge. Science as Culture 7(1):33–67.

Wilkins, David E.
1997   American Indian Sovereignty and the Masking of Justice. Austin: University of Texas Press.

Wilkins, David E., and K. Tsianina Lomawaima
2001   Uneven Ground: American Indian Sovereignty and Federal Law. Norman: University of Oklahoma Press.

Wolfe, Patrick
2001   Land, Labor and Difference: Elementary Structures of Race. American Historical Review 106(3):866–905.
2007   *Corpus Nullius*: The Exception of Indians and Other Aliens in US Constitutional Discourse. Postcolonial Studies 10(2):127 - 151.

Yasaitis, Kelly E.
2005   NAGPRA: A Look Back through the Litigation. Journal of Land, Resources, and Environmental Law 25:259–285.

Yazzie, Robert
1998   Navajo Peacemaking: Implications for Adjudication-Based Systems of Justice. Contemporary Justice Review 1:123–131.

Yellow Bird, Pemina, and Kathryn Milun
1994   Interrupted Journeys: The Cultural Politics of Indian Reburial. *In* Displacements: Cultural Identities in Question. A. Bammer, ed. Pp. 3–24. Bloomington and Indianapolis: Indiana University Press.

Zehr, Howard, and Barb Toews
2004   Critical Issues in Restorative Justice. Monsey, NY: Criminal Justice Press.

Zimmerman, Larry J.
2005   Public Heritage, a Desire for a "White" History for America, and Some Impacts of the Kennewick Man/Ancient One Decision. International Journal of Cultural Property 12(2):265–274.

Zion, James W.
1998   The Use of Custom and Legal Tradition in the Modern Justice Setting. Contemporary Justice Review 1:133–148.
2006   Justice as Phoenix: Traditional Indigenous Law, Restorative Justice, and the Collapse of the State. *In* Native Americans and the Criminal Justice System. J. I. Ross and L. A. Gould, eds. Pp. 51–65. Boulder, CO: Paradigm Publishers.

Zion, James W., and Robert Yazzie
1997   Indigenous Law in North America in the Wake of Conquest. Boston College International and Comparative Law Review 10(1):55–84.

Index

A

aboriginal justice. *See* indigenous justice
Aboriginal title, 46–47, 53, 64, 69
Allendoerfer, Judge James, 7, 12–14,
    16–18, 20–23
alternative justice. *See* restorative jus-
    tice. *See also* indigenous justice
Ancient One. *See* Kennewick Man
apartheid. *See* race (in Musqueam Park
    dispute)

B

banishment: as assertion of sovereignty,
    15–16, 22; authenticity and,
    8, 12, 14; failure of, 8, 17–18,
    23. *See also* indigenous justice,
    restorative justice
BCCA. *See* British Columbia Court of
    Appeal
Belleau, Charlene, 26
Belleau, Marilyn 25–28, 40–43
BIA. *See* Bureau of Indian Affairs
Bonnichsen, Robson, 72, 75–76
Bridging the Cultural Divide: discourses
    of, 29–37, 43; Royal Com-
    mission on Aboriginal Peoples
    report, 29–32, 35–37, 43
British Columbia Court of Appeal,
    24–25, 35, 40–43
Bureau of Indian Affairs, 12, 19–21

C

Cariboo Indian Residential School, 24,
    37, 39
Catholic Church. *See* Roman Catholic
    Church
Caucasoid. *See* whiteness (Caucasoid/
    Caucasian, Kennewick Man as)
Caucasian. *See* whiteness (Caucasoid/
    Caucasian, Kennewick Man as)

Chatters, James, 71, 75–81
consent: agency and, 39, 41–42; colo-
    nial history and, 35–37, 39–43;
    legal construction of, 34–35,
    39–43; residential schools and,
    35, 37–39, 41–43; in sexual
    violence cases, 35; temporality
    of, 35–36, 40–42
Crow Dog. See *Ex parte Crow Dog*
cultural relativism, 3–4
culturalization. *See* race (culturaliza-
    tion of)
customary law. *See* indigenous justice

D

difference. *See* indigeneity
docile body, concept of, 38–39

E

Eagle and the Raven, The, 14
ethnic cleansing by fiscal means. *See*
    race (in Musqueam Park dispute)
Ex parte Crow Dog, 19
Ex parte Tiger, 20

F

forensic facial reconstruction. *See*
    Kennewick Man (forensic facial
    reconstruction of)
Findlay, Kerry-Lynne, 45, 58
Five Races of Man, 75
Foucault. *See* docile body (concept of)

G

genetic indigeneity. *See* indigeneity
    (genetic)
Genographic Project, 87
George, Pamela, 36
Gonthier, Justice Charles. *See* Supreme
    Court of Canada

Guthrie, Adrian, 7, 12–18, 20, 22–23

H

healing, discourses of, 11, 26. *See also* healing circle
healing circle: authenticity and, 32–34; feminist critiques of, 25, 27–28; as indigenous space, 24–28, 31–36, 43–44; as restorative justice, 25–26. *See also* restorative justice
HGDP. *See* Human Genome Diversity Project
Human Genome Diversity Project, 76, 82

I

Indian Act, 54–55, 57, 60–61
indigenous legal identity: 4, 52–53, 60, 73–74, 75, 82. *See also* indigeneity
Indian Reorganization Act, 20–21
Indian remains: history of, 74–75, 86–87; legislative history of. *See* Native American Graves and Repatriation Act
Indian title. *See* Aboriginal title
indigeneity: in the courtroom, 1–2, 6; definition of, 1, 4–5; erasure of, 5, 35–36, 42–44; genetic, 5, 73–74, 82–85, 88; legal production of 1–2, 4–6, 8, 25, 42–44, 83–88; politics of recognition and, 2–3, 20, 30–31, 69–70, 88; property and. *See* property (difference and); race and, 4, 42, 50, 52–53, 60–61, 72–73, 77, 80–81, 82–83, 87–88. *See also* race, whiteness; science and, 86–88. *See also* race (and science)
indigenous justice: as assertion of self-determination, 11, 28–29, 43; as critique of Western jurisprudence, 10–11; critiques of, 10–11, 32; culturalist discourses and, 5, 7, 8, 10, 14, 23, 29–34, 43; difference and, 10–12, 29–31, 34, 44; history of, 19–20, 28–31; legacy of colonialism and, 9–11, 23, 31–32; in Native North America, 8–12, 25–28; as postcolonial critique, 18–19, 28–29, 31. *See also* restorative justice

J

James, Diana Wynne, 13, 16–17
James, Rudy, 7–8, 12–18, 20–21

K

Kennewick Man: age of, 71–72, 77, 82–83, 86–87; as *corpus nullius*, 88; "folk heredity" and, 78; forensic facial reconstruction of, 78–81; lack of viable DNA and, 73–74, 80, 83–87; media representations of, 72, 78–81, 87; racial categorization of, 71–73, 76–77, 79–81, 83
Klawock Cooperative Association, 12–13, 15
Kuye di' Kuiu Kwaan Tribal Court, 7, 8, 12–17, 22–23. *See also* indigenous justice

L

landscape, concept of, 46, 48–49. *See also* Musqueam Park (as landscape)
leasehold reserve land. *See* property (leasehold reserve land as *sui generis* legal category of). *See also* property (difference and)
leaseholders. *See* settler societies (leaseholders as settler society)
legal anthropology, 8–9
Luna, Judge Douglas, 20–21

M

Magee, Michael, 12
Major Crimes Act, 19
Manitoba Justice Inquiry, 28–29
McClelland, Tom, 78–81
Morton, Samuel, 75–76
Musqueam Indian Band, 45, 46–48, 55–60
Musqueam Park: creation of, 53–55; emergence of, 54–55; as Indian land, 5, 45–50, 52–54, 57, 59–60, 64–70; as landscape, 46, 48–49, 53–56; lease terms 46–47, 49, 54–55; location of, 45, 54–55; resettlement of, 48, 51–53

N

NAGPRA. *See* Native American Graves and Repatriation Act

Native American Graves and Repatriation Act, 71–72, 74–75, 80–85, 87–88

O

O'Connor, Bishop Hubert Patrick, 25–28, 31–33, 34, 36–37, 40–43
Oppal, Justice Wally, 34–35, 40–43

P

Pacific Spirit Regional Park, 55–56
Picard, Jean-Luc. *See* Kennewick Man (forensic facial reconstruction of). *See also* whiteness (Caucasoid/Caucasian, Kennewick Man as)
politics of recognition. *See* indigeneity, politics of recognition and
property: 1, 5; colonization and, 50–54, 73; concepts of, 45–46, 67. *See also* Musqueam Park (as landscape); difference and, 46–48, 57–62, 63–64; Indian land as, 45–49, 52–54, 56–60, 64–70. *See also* Musqueam Park (as Indian land); intellectual, 9; leasehold reserve land as *sui generis* legal category of, 47, 54, 64–69; private, 52, 63–64, 67; valuation of in Musqueam Park, 49–50, 56, 64–68; whiteness and. *See* whiteness (property and)

Q

Quantz, Ernie, 24–26

R

race: culturalization of, 4, 51, 60–61; history of in British Columbia, 50–54; Kennewick Man and. *See* Kennewick Man (racial categorization of); in Musqueam Park dispute, 50–54, 56–62; science and, 51–52, 72–73, 74–78, 82–83. *See also* Kennewick Man (forensic facial reconstruction of)
racial science. *See* race (science and)
racialization. *See* race. *See also* whiteness.
reserves: history of in BC, 53–54; creation of Musqueam Indian Reserve, 54–55. *See also* Musqueam Park, property

(leasehold reserve land as *sui generis* category of)
residential schools: abuse at, 25, 27, 32–33, 37–39; effects of, 31, 35, 37–39, 41–44; history of, 37–39, 41; lawsuits involving, 33
resettlement. *See* Musqueam Park (resettlement of). *See also* settler societies
restorative justice: alternative dispute resolution (ADR), 10, 28; as critique of criminal justice system, 10–11, 15, 18, 22; critiques of, 10–11, 25, 27–28; family group conferencing (FGC), 10, 28; indigenous communities and, 9–11, 25, 27–29; violence against women and, 27–29; *See also* indigenous justice
Roberts, Simon, 7, 12–18, 20, 22–23
Roman Catholic Church, 25, 27, 32–33, 37–38
Royal Commission on Aboriginal Peoples. *See* Bridging the Cultural Divide (Royal Commission on Aboriginal Peoples report)

S

settler societies: cultural discourses of, 56–62; law and, 2, 18–20, 26, 29–34, 36–37, 46–49, 51–54, 63–64, 67–69, 82–83; leaseholders as settler society, 46–48, 49, 53, 56–62, 69–70
Stewart, Patrick. *See* Kennewick Man (forensic facial reconstruction of). *See also* whiteness (Caucasoid/Caucasian, Kennewick Man as)
Supreme Court of Canada, 45–49, 54, 64, 66–70

T

temporality of consent. *See* consent, temporality of
terra nullius, 52, 88
Tlingit-Haida Central Council, 12, 20
Townsend, Jim, 13
tribal justice. *See* indigenous justice
tribal law. *See* indigenous justice

U

University Endowment Lands (UEL), 55–56

University of British Columbia (UBC), 55

V

violence against women: colonialism and, 29, 39–40; sexual and domestic violence, 27–29, 35

W

Wheeler-Howard Act. *See* Indian Reorganization Act

whiteness: *See also* race, settler societies; Caucasoid/Caucasian, Kennewick Man as, 71–72, 76–77, 77–81. *See also* Kennewick Man (racial categorization of); indigeneity and, 25, 39–40, 42–43, 82–83. *See also* indigeneity (race and); property and, 50–51

Whittlesey, Tim, 12, 14, 18